# PUB WA

# IN KE

## Forty Circular Walks

## Around Kent Inns

**Other publications in the series**

Pub Walks in Dorset
Forty More Pub Walks in Dorset
Mike Power Pub Walks along the Dorset Coast
Pub Walks in Hampshire
More Pub Walks in Hampshire
Pub Walks in West Sussex
Pub Walks in East Sussex
Pub Walks in Devon
Pub Walks in Somerset
Pub Walks in The New Forest
Pub Walks in Hardy's Wessex
Pub Walks in North Surrey
Pub Walks in South Surrey
40 More Pub Walks in Surrey

1st edition – published May 1994
2nd edition – published June 2011

**ACKNOWLEDGEMENTS**

38 of the walks in this book were originally researched by David Hancock but updated in 2010 by John Quarendon who has included two new walks, at Hadlow and Warehorne respectively.



ISBN 978-1-898073-37-6



**Publishers Note**
Whilst every care has been taken to ensure that all the information given in this book is correct, errors will occur due to many factors. Path are sometimes re-routed after research, stiles can replace gates and visa versa but sadly the pubs themselves can change hands or worse close for good. Neither the publishers nor the printers can accept responsibility for any inaccuracies.

Power Publications
1 Clayford Avenue Ferndown
Dorset, BH22 9PQ
powerpublications@hotmail.com

Front cover: The Plough, Stalisfield Green
Photos: Bonita Toms and John Quarendon
Printed by Pardy & Son (Printers) Ltd., Ringwood Hants

# INTRODUCTION

This collection of 40 circular walks explores deep into the heart of the beautiful Kentish countryside – The Garden of England – and discovers a diverse landscape with a rich heritage. The chalk escarpment and rolling downland of the North Downs and fertile slopes of the greensand ridge characterise the high points of the county, the latter providing panoramic views across the level, sheep-grazed pastures of the Weald to the undulating ridges of the High Weald and the Sussex border. Kent's coastal scenery is just as varied, ranging from the spectacular white cliffs of Dover with views of France to wild and desolate marshland along the estuaries of the Swale, Medway and Thames.

Dotted across the area are hop fields, orchards, woodland and oast houses, fine medieval manor houses and a wealth of unspoilt villages that preserve ancient black and white timbered, weather boarded or tile-hung cottages, picturesque churches and an excellent choice of traditional inns. This book includes 40 of the best chosen for their charm, their location and proximity to lovely walks. No charge is made for inclusion in this guide.

Kent is blessed with a superb network of well-marked and well maintained footpaths, thanks to the efforts of the County Council and the ever increasing popularity of this healthy leisure activity. Four long distance footpaths – North Downs Way/Pilgrims Way, Greensand Way, Wealdway and Saxon Shore Way – cross the county and many of the walks in this guide incorporate sections of these scenic trails. The walks are all circular, ranging between 2 to 7 miles in length, described in detail with an accompany sketch map and listing points of interest nearby and on the routes. The walks are kept short to appeal to families and are planned to start and finish at the pub, although it is possible to start anywhere along the route. If you are planning to use the pub car park it is only courteous to ask the landlord's permission first.

It is advisable to take with you the appropriate Ordnance Survey map which is indicated at the beginning of each walk, along with the exact reference of the start point and postcode should you have a sat. nav. The map number refers to the 1:25,000 – 2 ½ inch to the mile Explorer series. If you should find any of the paths obstructed in any way please inform the Public Rights of Way Dept, at Kent County Council Telephone: 01622 696740

We know that walking is extremely good for us and the best way to explore the countryside, but a few simple rules must be observed. Try to wear suitable clothing that befits the season and weather conditions. It is a good idea in summer to take a pair of trousers if wearing shorts as many paths can become overgrown with nettles and brambles. A walking stick is ideal for clearing the way ahead, testing for stability of the ground and can be waved to deter animals. Waterproof, well treaded boots are essential, a compass can be useful and if walking into the evening it is a good idea to carry a torch. Always take care on country lanes without pavements and where safe to do so try to walk facing the on-coming traffic.

Wherever you go always remember the country code. Guard against all fires, fasten all gates if found shut, keep dogs under control and always on a lead where there is livestock, keep to the path across farm land, take all litter home, respect wildlife and do not pick or dig up wild flowers.

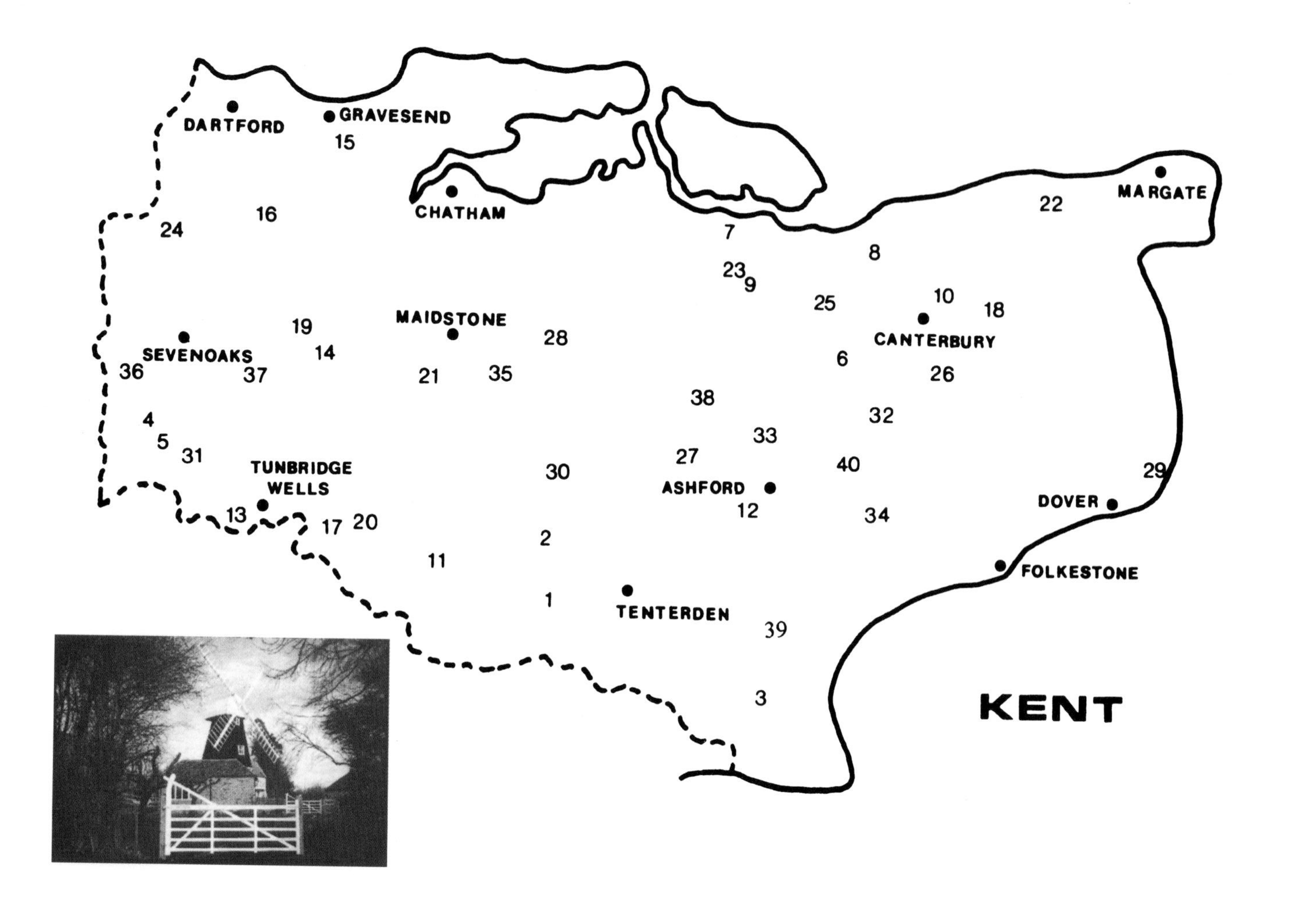
KENT
DARTFORD
GRAVESEND
CHATHAM
MARGATE
MAIDSTONE
SEVENOAKS
CANTERBURY
TUNBRIDGE WELLS
ASHFORD
DOVER
FOLKESTONE
TENTERDEN

## Index



**Tourist Information centres**

| | | | |
|---|---|---|---|
| Ashford | 01233 629165 | Herne Bay | 01227 361911 |
| Canterbury | 01227 766567 | Maidstone | 01622 673581 |
| Dartford | 01322 343243 | Sevenoaks | 01732 450305 |
| Dover | 01304 205108 | Tonbridge | 01732 770929 |
| Faversham | 01795 534542 | Tunbridge Wells | 01892 515675 |
| Gravesend | 01474 337600 | Whitstable | 01227 275482 |

**Walk No. 1**

# The King William IV, Benenden

Located in the heart of the village, close to its large attractive green complete with cricket pitch and church is the King William IV, an excellent unspoilt village local that dates back to the 16th-century and boasts an intriguing history. It was originally a chapel, providing a resting place for weary pilgrims on their way to Canterbury. It obtained its licence in the 18th-century and soon became one of the haunts of the infamous Hawkhurst gang, a band of smugglers that terrorised the area. The relaxing cosy lounge bar boasts a huge inglenook fireplace with log fire and seating, exposed beams and furnished pews and some pine and cricket tables. Behind the car park is a large garden dotted with benches and fruit trees and a children's play area.

Owned by Shepherd Neame the pub offers their ales, usually Spitfire, Master Brew and Canterbury Jack with seasonal variations like Early Bird and Late Red. There is also an extensive wine list.

The restaurant, with its inset fireplace and exposed floorboards, makes a pleasant space to enjoy a lunchtime or evening meal and may be hired for private functions. Available 12 noon till 3 pm and 6 till 9pm, Monday to Saturday and 12 noon till 9 pm on Sunday when a traditional roast is available. A past "Restaurant of the Year", the inn serves traditional home-cooked food using local produce and includes some Mediterranean influences reflecting the chef's experience of cooking abroad. The menu changes regularly according to the season, with sandwiches and King William "classics" and a children's menu. The staff offer to meet any special dietary requirements if given notice. Also regular gourmet nights.

Opening times all day 11.30 till 11 pm seven days a week.

Dogs are welcome in the bar and garden on a lead but not in the restaurant.

Telephone: 01580 240636.

Village and pub are located on the B2086 between Rolvenden and Cranbrook, 5 miles west of Tenterden. Postcode: TN17 4DJ.

Approx. distance of walk: 4½ miles. OS Map No. 125 TQ 808/329.

Parking is limited at the inn, but there is space by the village green near the church.

*A delightful varied, undulating and scenic walk along well waymarked field paths and woodland tracks in a very unspoilt rural part of Kent. The going can be wet and muddy after rain so good waterproof footwear is essential especially during the winter. Of interest nearby is the fascinating collection of historic vehicles at Rolvenden.*

1. Turn right on leaving the pub, then right again beside the village green to the church. Bear right with the footpath fingerpost, then keep left along the metalled pathway and descend via three wooden gates to a road. Keep left along the verge, then shortly climb the stile beside the driveway to Woodside. Head half-right on a defined path across a field to an arrowed stile preceeding woodland. Follow a good path to a junction of tracks and cross straight over onto a wide track through the wood. Keep ahead where the track bears sharp right and follow footpath 333 downhill to a stile on the woodland edge. Proceed along the right-hand edge of a field parallel to a brook and soon climb a stile by a gate onto a lane.

2. Turn left, then keep right at a T-junction and shortly bear off left uphill. Pass Barnhill Cottage, then look out for a waymarked stile on your left beside a gate. Proceed straight ahead uphill across a pasture and pass through a yellow marked field gate near a house. Continue along the field edge, pass through a further gate and maintain direction to a metal gate in the field corner. Bear right into Ramsden Farm, keep ahead across the crossroads of concrete farm tracks, then curve right behind barn and turn left with yellow waymarker on telegraph pole to

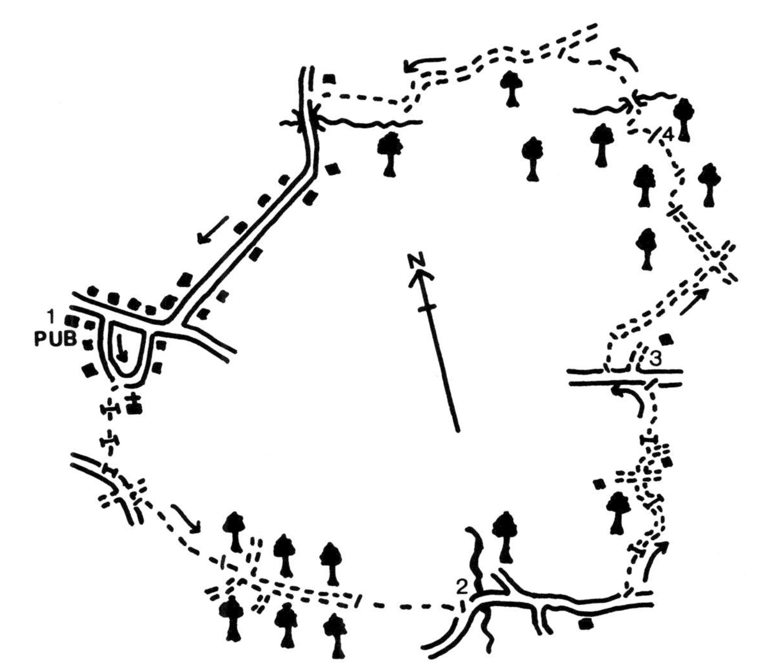

a gate. Proceed half-right towards a disused windmill, soon to pick up the grassy path in the field corner that leads to a stile and the B2086, near the old windmill.

3. Turn left, then in a little way cross the road and a waymarked stile beside a driveway. Bear slightly right towards a line of poplar trees and climb a stile into an orchard. Turn right along its edge, shortly to bear right with yellow markers through a gate way into the adjacent field. Keep left along the grassy field edge then at a crossing of tracks turn left with an arrow along the left-hand edge of an orchard and downhill into a coniferous woodland, eventually reaching a stile. Follow the grassy track which curves right to a further gate and stile and resume your route through woodland.

4. Climb a stile on the woodland fringe, bear left then right downhill and shortly cross a footbridge over a stream. Keep left, cross a stile, then turn left uphill along the edge of a field to a waymarked stile in the hedge and turn left along a wide established track way. Remain on this track, skirting ponds and woodland, then parallel with a stream – your route can be very wet and muddy – to a narrow lane. Turn left and follow it into Benenden, turning right at the B-road in the village back to the pub.

Rolvenden Mill on the B2086 between Benenden and Rolvenden

**Walk No. 2**

# The Three Chimneys, Biddenden

This real gem of a country pub, dating from 1420, was originally a half-timbered farmhouse before becoming an ale house during the 1800's to serve the workers on the neighbouring hop picking farms. The name relates to its location rather than to the number of chimneys on the building, as it is the corruption of the French 'trois chemins' or 'the three ways'. During the Napoleonic wars, French officers were held prisoners at nearby Sissinghurst Castle, but were allowed to go for country walks and the junction of the three roads where the pub stands was their parole limit – hence the name. The unassuming façade hides a classic interior that has been virtually untouched over the centuries. A warren of rooms feature low beams hung with hops, flagstone floors and wood panelled walls. The atmosphere is warm, welcoming and traditional with a delightful mix of rustic old furniture – wooden pews and benches, sturdy tables – blazing winter log fires and evening candlelight. The small splendidly traditional public bar is dominated by a vast inglenook fireplace. At the rear is the Garden Room, which is furnished with a collection of old fashioned tables and chairs and overlooks the garden.

This excellent free house dispenses six ales which may include Adnams and Brakespear Bitters, Marston's Pedigree, Wadworth 6X, Old Speckled Hen and Harveys Old Ale as well as the local Biddenden cider and an interesting list of wines.

Food service is 12 - 2 pm and 6 - 9 pm weekdays, 12 - 2.30 pm - and 6 - 9.30 pm at weekends. The menu changes daily and appears on blackboards. A typical selection may include carrot and orange soup, buttered haddock pâté, duck or chestnut mousse followed by beef and pigeon casserole, partridge and apricot pie, steak and oyster pie, Kentish lamb plus vegetarian choices.

Weekday opening times 11.30 till 3 pm, (4 pm Saturday) and 5.30 till 11 pm, Sunday 12 noon till 4 pm and 6 till 10.30 pm.

Children are welcome in the garden room and dogs allowed on leads.

Telephone: 01580 291472.

## Walk No. 2

Pub is located just off the A262 between Biddenden and Sissinghurst, 1 mile west of Biddenden. Postcode: TN27 8LW.

Approx. distance of walk: 4 miles. OS Map No. 137 827/388.

There is a large car park to the front of the inn.

*An enjoyable level walk along established tracks, peaceful country lanes and field paths with the opportunity to visit the splendid colourful gardens of Sissinghurst Castle (NT). The Tudor mansion and gardens were restored by Sir Harold Nicholson and the writer Vita Sackville-West and are a delight to explore in both spring and summer (open April to mid October). Some of the tracks can be very wet and muddy during the winter months. Further attractions in the locality include the attractive weather boarded village of Cranbrook with its fine working 'smock mill' (open). The small town of Tenterden is close by and is the beginning of the Kent and East Sussex Railway, a delightful 7-mile steam journey through the Weald.*

1. Leave the pub car park at the exit by the pub sign and turn right along the narrow lane. Keep left on reaching a junction, pass the entrance to Bettenham Manor, then where the lane curves right, bear off left beside a metal barrier onto a wide track way. Gently descend and cross the bridge across Hammer Stream and continue towards Sissinghurst Castle.

2. On reaching the complex of buildings with the shop/barn in front of you, bear left then right with restaurant to your right and follow the metalled track past the farm shop onto a driveway towards a house. At the house turn sharp right onto an established tree-lined pathway (can be very wet and muddy) and gently descend, eventually reaching a track beside a house. Follow the driveway to a junction of lanes.

3. Proceed straight across, waymarked Sand Lane then just beyond metal barns (Brisenden Farm) on your left, pass through green double gates to the right onto a concrete drive. Pass a barn, then bear half-right onto a worn path across a field to a stile in a hedge. Continue across pasture to a further stile beside a tree, then proceed ahead to cross a footbridge over a stream. Keep left along the field edge, cross a plank bridge in the field corner and turn right onto a wide grassy path. Where the track curves right cross the waymarked footbridge ahead, then pass through scrub and follow the worn path to a stile and a lane. Climb the stile opposite, step over a covered wire fence and follow it left-handed. Shortly to bear slightly right to a stile. Maintain direction behind bungalows to a further stile and turn left along the lane back to the pub.

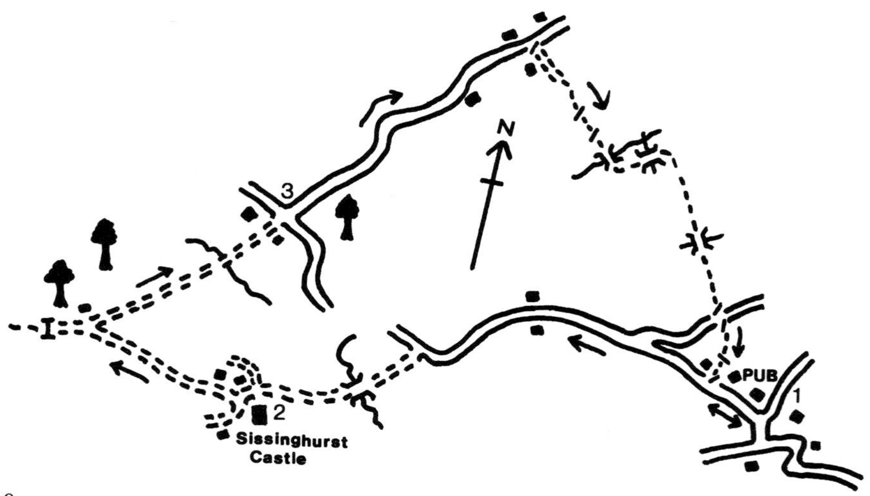

# The Woolpack, Brookland

Originally a beacon keeper's cottage dating from 1410, this low, white-painted pub is tucked away along a lane, isolated among open sheep pastures and overlooking a reed-fringed dyke. It has been a pub for over 400 years and was a well known smuggling haunt when gangs would use the Romney Marsh coast to trade wool for rum and brandy brought over from France. The pub has featured in many films as a smugglers inn and the old spinning wheel used to divide up the smugglers' contraband is still visible. Beyond the old worn brick entrance and low doorway lies the splendid main bar, which oozes atmosphere and charm. A roaring winter fire burns in the massive inglenook which has seating for those frozen to the bone and a head cracking low beamed ceiling awaits unsuspecting customers. A quarry-tiled floor is topped with rustic benches, long tables and a mix of stools, wheelback chairs and pub tables. A collection of water jugs hangs above the bar and various pieces of copper and brass adorn the walls.

This Shepherd Neame pub dispenses well conditioned Master Brew, Spitfire and either their Early Bird or Porter on hand pump. Summer sipping can be enjoyed in the waterside garden.

Bar food is served daily between 12 noon and 2.30 pm and from 6 till 9 pm. Weekend food served 12 noon till 9 pm. The short selection of good value, home-cooked dishes include soup, shepherds pie, lasagne, chilli, steak pie and various steaks. A daily specials board may list liver and bacon or a roast. Snacks include ploughman's, sandwiches, filled jacket potatoes and garlic bread.

Weekday opening times are from 11 am till 3 pm and 6 till 11 pm, Saturday 11 till 11 pm, Sunday 12 noon till 10.30 pm

Children are most welcome and high chairs are provided. Dogs are allowed inside on a lead.

Telephone: 01797 344321.

## Walk No. 3

Brookland is located on the A259 New Romney to Rye road on the Romney Marsh. The pub lies 1 mile south-west of the village towards Rye, just off the A259. Postcode: TN29 9TJ.

Approx. distance of walk: 3½ miles. OS Map No. 125 TQ978/245.

There is a car park at the pub and space alongside the lane.

*A short level stroll through sheep filled pastures, open arable land, across dykes and along quiet narrow lanes. Due to the low lying nature of the land it can be wet underfoot and hard going if recently ploughed. The splendid ancient church of Saint Augustine in Brookland, with its curious wooden belfry, is one of the most attractive churches in Romney Marsh and is the focus of this walk.*

1. Leave the pub, turn left along the lane across the dyke and shortly bear off left with fingerpost and drop down into pasture. Climb the metal gate, then bear diagonally right through pasture, crossing a dyke soon to reach a stile and lane close to an isolated cottage. Turn right, then in a few yards climb the waymarked stile left and keep to the left-hand field hedge to a wooden footbridge. Continue across an open field to a stile and bear half-left across a further field to a stile in the far corner and enter a paddock. Proceed left-handed in front of a cottage to a stile and continue to a swing gate onto a lane. Turn right, following the lane left to visit the unusual historic church of St Augustine in Brookland village.

2. Retrace your steps across the paddock, path waymarked to Fairfield. Beyond the second stile bear right into a grassy field and keep to its left-hand edge, passing an old white shed. On reaching the field corner, bear half-right across an open crop field to a fingerpost, a stile and the A road. Turn left and soon cross over to take the arrowed, well defined path that heads half-left across an open field and through a gateway to reach a footbridge over a dyke.

3. Beyond the dyke turn left along the field edge, ignore the arrowed path right and continue to a stile and lane. Turn right and remain on the lane as it bears left, soon to pass The Laurels and a farm complex to a T-junction of lanes. Turn left and follow the lane with good open views to the main road. Taking great care, turn right along the road to a sharp right-hand bend, then bear off left along a lane for a short distance back to the pub.

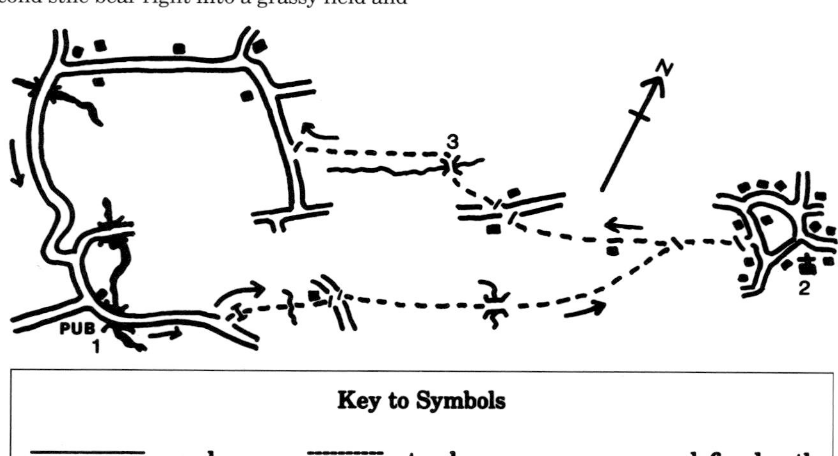

Warming winter log fire in The Woolpack

The interesting church of St. Augustine in Brookland

**Walk No. 4**

# The Castle Inn, Chiddingstone

Located opposite the parish church in a unique, unspoilt row of Tudor timbered houses, this historic tile-hung inn with its leaded casement windows and projecting gables is, like the rest of the village, owned by the National Trust. This magnificent building is referred to in 1420 and was then known as Waterslip House. It was bought in 1712 by Thomas Weller, a tailor, who with his brother started the inn about 1730 and some 270 years later it is still one of the main centres of village life and an extremely popular refreshment stop for visiting tourists. Despite its popularity, this fine inn has remained delightfully untouched over the years, comprising two traditional and atmospheric bars. The public bar is splendidly rustic with a quarry tiled floor - no problem with muddy boots, a heavily beamed ceiling, old brick fireplace with wood burner and simple wall bench seating. It is a true locals bar. Those seeking extra comfort can relax in the cosy, beamed and carpeted saloon bar. Sunny summer days can be enjoyed on the vine-covered terrace and in the pretty rear garden, complete with small pool, fountain, flower borders and a neat bench-filled lawn.

The pub is a freehouse and the well stocked bar dispenses Larkins Traditional and Harveys Best on hand pump as well as a range of malt whiskies and a choice of over 150 wines from a wide-ranging list.

Good bar food is served all week. Lunch time favourites include homemade soup, sandwiches, fresh pastas and traditional shepherds' pie and a blackboard offers daily specials. Treacle tart is a popular pudding and the cheese board is served with homemade chutney.

The inn is open every day all day starting with coffee at 10.30 am and alcoholic drinks from 11 am till 11 pm, Sunday 12 noon till 10.30 pm.

Both dogs and children are welcome inside.

Telephone: 01892 870247.

## Walk No. 4

Village is situated 1 mile south of the B2027 Penshurst to Edenbridge road. Postcode: TN8 7AH.

Approx: distance of walk: 5½ miles. OS Map No. 147 TQ 500/452.

Parking is limited at the pub to spaces along the village lane.

*A most enjoyable fairly level ramble, affording good countryside views making an ideal walk for the whole family. Part of the walk passes through the grounds of Hever Castle, an enchanting, double-moated, 13th-century castle that was the childhood home of Anne Boleyn (open daily mid March to early November). Also open to the public (April to October) is Chiddingstone Castle, a 17th-century house displaying fine paintings and Egyptian and Oriental antiquities.*

1. From the inn, turn right along the lane and take the first footpath right if wishing to see 'Chiding Stone' – legend has it that was a natural platform for a preacher to address his followers. The main route follows the second path right, just beyond a driveway. Stay on the path ahead to cross two stiles into a field, then drop down to a stile beside a copse directly ahead. Keep to the right and pass through the copse to an open gateway. Cross a track, then a stile on the right and follow the path through a farm complex to meet a farm road which bears right between cottages.

2. Turn left onto a private road (vehicles only) and go through a small gate on the right to join a fenced bridleway. Continue along the bridleway and look for a stile on the right between two large steel gates and enter woodland. Follow track downhill, cross a footbridge over a stream, waymarked 'Eden Valley Walk, and proceed with markers over a stile and along a fenced track to a further stile and road. Cross over and keep to the footpath soon to pass to the right of a farm and houses eventually reaching the drive to Hever Castle. Go through the gate on the right, follow the drive then the footpath over a footbridge to another fenced path and shortly pass through Hever churchyard to the road.

3. Turn left, then where the road veers sharp right, keep straight on to pass the school and join a footpath which leads to a road. Turn left then in a few yards climb the waymarked stile and follow the direction of the marker to the left-hand corner of the field by a pond and enter another field. Continue ahead along the left-hand side of the field to cross two stiles into the next field. Keeping to the left, continue on to cross another two stiles and head for a stile in the top right hand corner of the field onto a road. Turn right, then left at a T-junction, eventually reaching a T-junction opposite Wildeness Farm.

4. Turn right and upon reaching a "give-way" sign, turn left onto a track (Footpath sign). Follow this established track through woodland with several iron gates to join a fenced track (good views). On reaching an iron gate and stile by the private road used on the outward route, turn right and retrace your steps back to the Castle Inn.

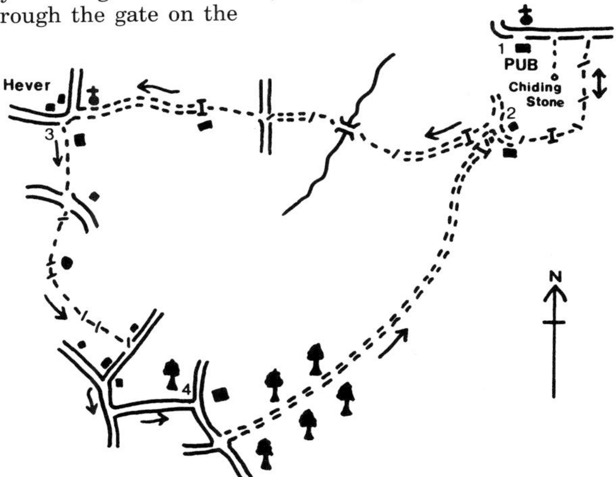

Walk No. 5

# The Rock Inn, Chiddingstone Hoath

Hidden away in the depths of unspoilt countryside, this attractive, creeper and rose adorned brick and tile hung building dates back to 1510. For many years it was part of the Hever estate and has been used as a slaughter house, among other things, before becoming an ale house serving the estate workers. Old world character and charm fills the unadulterated main bar which boasts a low, oak beamed ceiling, an original uneven red-brick floor – no problem with muddy boots – exposed wall beams, leaded windows and a splendid inglenook with a roaring woodburner. Old wooden casks serve as tables and seating includes tapestry covered stools, padded bench seats and a comfortable worn leather chair which fronts the fire. Above this chair and mounted on the wall is a huge, menacing bull's head, the object of a local pub game, Ringing the Bull. Cream painted walls are hung with several prints and a collection of bank notes decorate the heavy beams. The adjacent, smaller and cosier bar is furnished with old church wall pews and red leatherette chairs and has a small brick fireplace. There is a secluded rear garden with picnic benches.

Since 1990 this rustic pub has been a freehouse. Two unusual wooden beer engines dispense Sharp's Doom Bar and local Larkins Bitter which is brewed a mile or so down the lane. They usually feature a second Larkins brew as a guest.

Food is available between 12 noon and 2.30 pm and from 7 till 9 pm. No evening food on Sunday when the pub closes at 5 pm. Only snacks available Monday lunch times. Home-cooked bar food is listed on a backboard menu above the bar and features daily-changing dishes as well as sound favourites. Choices include vegetable soup, cod and chips, ham, egg and chips, four types of ploughman's, lasagne, beef casserole, cottage pie, macaroni cheese, steak and kidney pie and winter game from local shoots. Separate sandwich board. Homemade puddings may include treacle tart, apple crumble and various sponges.

Weekday opening times are from 12 noon till 3 pm and 6 till 11 pm, the pub closes at 4 pm on Mondays.

Children are welcome and the garden is fenced and safe. Dogs are very welcome inside.

Telephone: 01892 870296.

## Walk No. 5

The pub is located at Hoath Corner between Chiddingstone and Hoath Corner, 3 mile west of Penshurst. Postcode: TN8 7BS.

Approx. distance of walk: 4½ miles. OS Map No. 147 TQ 498/431.

There is a small car park at the pub.

*A most enjoyable, scenic rural ramble on good paths, including the Sussex Border Path, and along short stretches of quiet country lanes. Generally easy going.*

1. From the pub turn left, then almost immediately right at a junction to join a narrow lane, passing Truggers Farms and shortly reach a T-junction. Cross over and pass through a waymarked metal gate onto a track beside a house. On reaching a metal gate climb the stile on the right into pasture and bear diagonally left downhill to a stile on the woodland fringe. Follow the narrow path along the woodland edge and shortly bear right into the wood, downhill to a footbridge over a stream. Climb a muddy bank to a stile, (path 534), enter pasture, keep left-handed beside woodland, then keep ahead at the end of the trees, uphill to a stile in the hedgerow.
2. Continue ahead, pass in front of cottages, bear left along driveway to cross a stile beside a gate and proceed downhill to a T-junction of tracks. Turn left, shortly pass Wickens Farm and bear right (yellow arrow, path 675) off the farm track to a waymarked stile. Follow narrow defined path beside wire fence to a fence stile then bear half-left across pasture to a further stile and continue along arrowed track way, downhill through Sandfields Farm to a lane. Keep left across the railway, pass Orchard Cottage, and shortly climb waymarked stile on your left, just before Moat Farm.
3. Proceed round a pond; keep right-handed through pasture to a small wooden gate and footbridge over a stream. Cross over and turn immediately left across a stile to join the well worn Sussex Border Path, parallel to the stream. Continue across three pastures via stiles and a footbridge, then walk beside a railway embankment, shortly to pass through a gate on the left and go under the railway. Bear half-right across meadow, over plank bridge to a stile near a footbridge with padlocked gate. Climb the stile, bear left to and negotiate a further footbridge over the stream. Leave Border Path, (arrowed right), keep straight ahead across meadow to a stile beside a pole fence, then cut the corner of a field to a further stile and proceed to the right of a barn and timbered house to a stile finally bearing right along the driveway to a lane.
4. Turn left, cross stream, then turn right through a gate onto a track and shortly bear off right with green arrow on tree to a metal gate. Head uphill, keep left of tree-ringed hollow to a stile and continue straight on to a further stile beside a horse jump. Soon bear right with the wide gallop, cross stile on the left and keep right-handed along field edge and around a pond to an arrowed stile and junction of paths. Climb the stile, keep right-handed along hedge to a further stile and a lane. Cross stile opposite and follow narrow path gently uphill beside fencing and driveway through scrub area to a stile. Keep ahead on grassy path between crop fields soon to bear right to a lane. Turn left and follow the lane back to the pub.

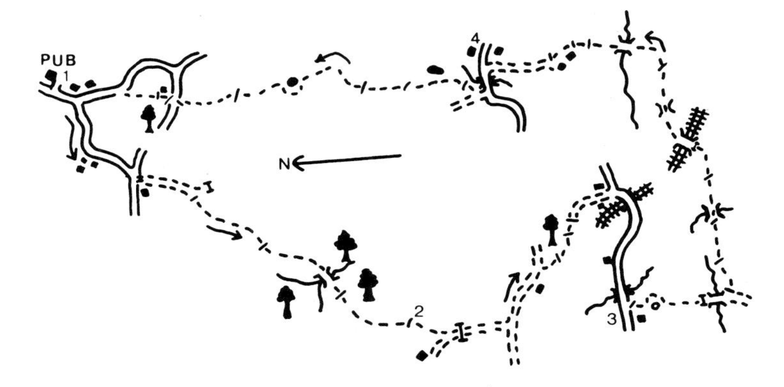

**Walk No. 6**

# The White Horse, Chilham

This attractive white painted, part-timbered pub nestles in the corner of one of the prettiest village squares in Kent and must claim to be the most photographed pub in the county. Built in 1422 as a thatched farm dwelling and later becoming an ale house used for festivals held in the adjacent church, it is, like the rest of the village, steeped in history. Refurbishments in 1956 revealed the skeletons of two men, possibly soldiers that were killed at the Battle of Chilham during the Wat Tyler rebellion of 1380. They are now buried in the churchyard. Also uncovered was the massive inglenook fireplace which was hidden by brick for over 200 years and displays a Lancastrian rose carved at the end of the mantel beam – a relic of the War of the Roses. The welcoming interior is open plan in style, around a central bar servery and features a carved beamed ceiling, some standing timbers, good winter log fires, comfortable sofas and dark wood tables and chairs. Attractive prints, paintings and local photographs adorn the walls and an unusual collection of hand bells hang from the ceiling in the food servery area. There is a pleasant walled garden shaded by cherry trees.

The well stocked bar dispenses Harveys Sussex, Shepherd Neame Master Brew and Greene King IPA as well as a fine selection of fruit wines from Chilham Vineyard and local pure apple juice.

Bar food is available from 12 noon till 2.45 pm (4 pm Sundays) and from 6.30 till 9 pm (except Sundays). The printed lunchtime menu list snacks such as homemade soup, salads, country platters and a range of sandwiches, while evening fare ranges from grilled trout, lemon sole bonne femme to venison in red wine and a selection of grills. Daily changing specials are written on a board above the bar and may include sausage casserole, sweet and sour turkey, macaroni cheese, vegetable lasagne and vegetable and lentil crumble.

Opening times are from 12 noon till 11 pm daily.

Children and dogs are allowed in the bar and garden.

This extremely popular pub has a number of letting rooms.

Telephone: 01227 730355.

Village lies just off the A28 and A252. 4 miles south-west of Canterbury. Postcode: CT4 8BY.

Approx. Distance of walk: 5 miles. OS Map No. 137 TR 068/536.

Park in village square or in the large free car park at the bottom of the village, off the A252.

*A delightful, gently undulating walk starting from one of Kent's most attractive villages, complete with fine castle grounds and raptor collection (open April to mid-October). It explores the scenic well waymarked tracks and woodland paths in the Stour Valley and is generally easy going, but the woodland ways can be muddy.*

1. From the pub turn left and leave the square, heading down the The Street past the post office. Keep left at a junction by the Woolpack, then bear right with the lane to the A28. Cross over onto a lane beside Ashford Road Service Station and join the Stour Valley Walk. Cross the level crossing, then the River Stour and pass to the right of Chilham Mill. Cross a stile and a further river channel, then bear left to join the narrow path beside the river. At a cross roads of paths, proceed straight across, then keep left around a field edge, gently climbing to a stile and track.

2. Turn left (good views along Stour Valley), ignore stile and waymarkers on your right and remain on the trackway to a metalled lane. Turn immediately right onto a waymarked path along the driveway to Mystole Farm. Pass the entrance to Mystole Court and turn right onto a gravel track towards farm buildings. Keep right at a fork and follow grass centred track uphill. On reaching a yellow topped post bear off right along the left-hand side of a fence, through a hedgerow, then along a track into mixed woodland.

3. Bear left to a T-junction of tracks, turn left, then immediately right onto a narrow path waymarked with blue markers. Turn right at the next junction and follow this established path to the woodland fringe. Follow blue arrow along the left-hand edge of an open field, soon to leave woodland edge on a defined grassy path between fields. At a marker post with arrows, bear right onto a wide track, shortly to bear right again to a stile preceeding woodland. Descend on a narrow path, keeping ahead at a crossroads of tracks, your path becoming hedged with good cameo views. Proceed straight on at a fork of paths, cross a stile and keep right downhill to merge with a track.

4. Bear right, pass beneath the railway, cross a stile beside a gate and follow driveway through farm complex to the main road. Turn left along the grass verge, shortly to cross over to a waymarked gate. Cross the footbridge over the Stour and bear diagonally right along a defined path across pasture. Cross a stile in the hedge on the left and head half-right across an open field to a fingerpost by some trees and join a narrow path to a lane opposite Orchard House. Turn right (North Downs Way) and follow it around the grounds of Chilham Castle, then up School Hill back into Chilham Square.

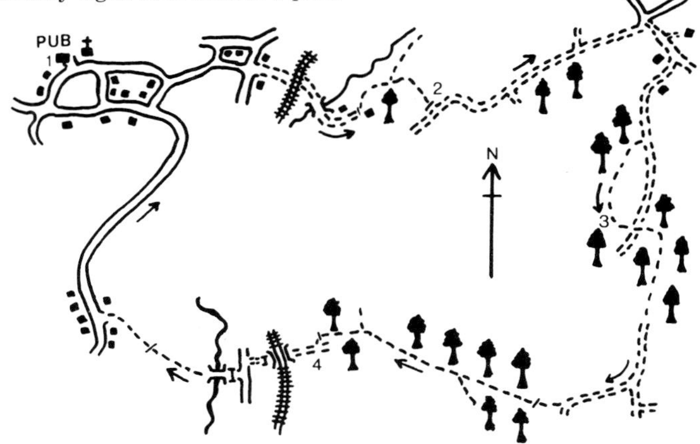

Walk No. 7

# The Ship, Conyer Quay

During the industrial revolution Conyer was known for its barge building some 500 believed to have been constructed here. Built in 1642, the Ship was originally a bakers one half becoming a blacksmiths. In 1802 Stephen Blaxford successfully applied for a licence but continued with the bakery in the other half. Because of its location it was also a notable smugglers' haunt. Located beside Conyer Creek, its front terrace overlooks the creek, marina and marshes. Recently renovated and extended the Ship now offers just the right atmosphere you would expect in a gastro pub with roaring fires, comfy chairs, an assortment of dark wood furniture, tables, stools and various church pews and benches.

The Ship is now a freehouse, the present owners Swale Marina having purchased the freehold from Enterprise Inns in February 2010 at which time they transformed the inn and re-opened in December 2010. Four real ales are the norm with Master Brew and Adams Bitter plus two other guest ales.

Food is available every day lunchtimes and evening. All the dishes are prepared and cooked on the premises with most of the ingredients sourced locally. 28-day matured beef is reared locally, bread is baked on the premises and all sauces and chutneys are made in the kitchens whilst the fish is obtained from local fishermen. The blackboard menu lists a variety of dishes such as mussels in Kentish cider, steak and ale pie, Conyer cheese/ham/ red onion and English mustard toasted sandwich with home made piccalilli, cold meat platter and local butchers sausages with crispy potato pancake and onion gravy.

Opening times Monday to Thursday 12 noon till 11 pm, Friday – Saturday 12 noon till 12 pm, Sunday 12 noon till 10.30 pm.

Children and dogs welcome.

Telephone: 01795 520881. www.shipinnconyer.co.uk.

Conyer Quay lies at the head of Conyer Creek, 2 miles north of the A2 at Teynham, between Sittingbourne and Faversham. Well signposted. Postcode: ME9 9HR.

Approx. distance of walk: 6½ miles. OS Map No. 149 TQ 962/648.

Parking is limited to the lane beside the pub.

*Although long, this level walk explores the Saxon Shore Way beside Conyer Creek and the Swale Estuary, returning along little used dead-end lanes. An excellent walk for bird lovers with the opportunity to see various waders, ducks, gulls and herons. Take you binoculars. In 2009 the Daily Telegraph selected this walk as one of the ten best in Great Britain.*

1. Leave the inn, turn right along the road and turn right where the road curves sharp left, onto a waymarked pitted track leading to Conyer Dock. Pass beside a Chandlery and continue across a boatyard to follow a track up onto a raised bank and path. Turn right, cross a stile and proceed on the delightful path – Saxon Shore Way – beside Conyer Creek. Cross a metal bridge by a sluice gate and remain on the raised bank, which soon curves left beside the Swale Estuary.

2. Continue for about ¾ mile alongside the estuary with good views across to the Isle of Sheppey and of the abundant birdlife. On reaching a wrecked hulk near an old concrete sluice, bear left off the bank onto a pitted track, following it inland past an old house. Shortly, curve left with the track, which soon becomes metalled and shortly pass Tonge Farm on your left. Proceed to a junction and turn left along a lane, arrowed to Blacketts.

3. At the end of the lane enter Blacketts farmyard, turning right between barns and silos onto a track which curves left, then right before heading across open farmland. Remain on the track to reach the raised creek side path beside Conyer Creek, at the sluice gate. Rejoin the path and retrace your steps back into Conyer and the pub.

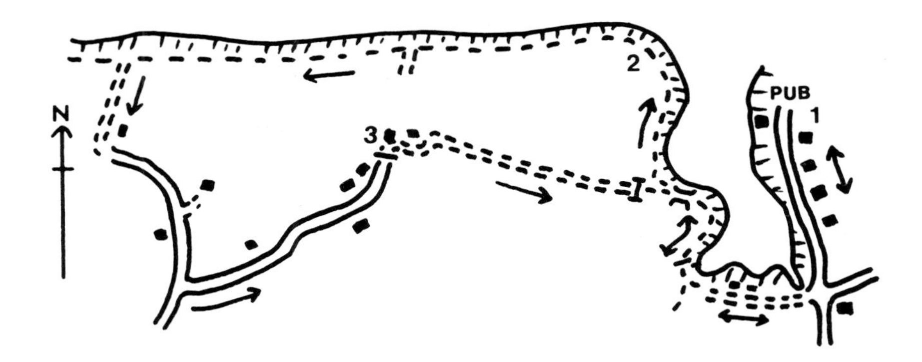


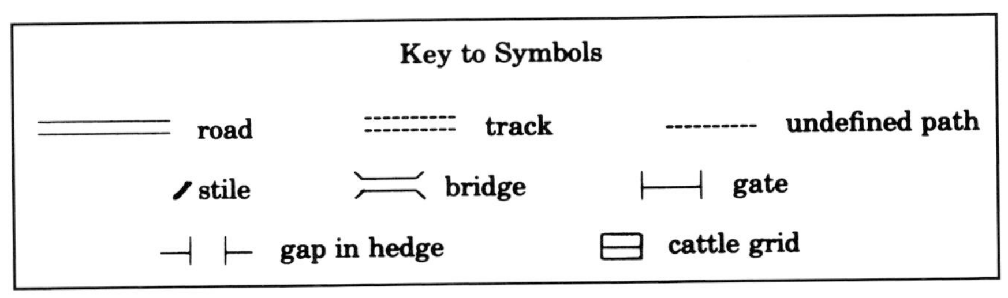

**Walk No. 8**

# The Dove, Dargate

Situated in the delightfully named Plum Pudding Lane beneath Blean Wood, this friendly and unpretentious honeysuckle and rose-clad brick pub was originally a thatched cottage built in 1570. It began as a home-brew house over 150 years ago and over the years has been altered and extended to the front leaving the old cottage unrecognisable to the rear. It is an idyllic summer pub with a peaceful mature garden complete with trees, dovecote, rockery and pool and masses of colourful cottage flowers. Pine abounds inside the homely rambling bar, from the floor and the wood-panelled walls to the rustic stripped and scrubbed pine tables and pews. An open fire warms the bar and old framed photographs of the pub and village in bygone days adorn the walls. A small family side room is furnished with modern pine and comfortable rush-seated ladder-backed chairs. The relaxing country atmosphere is enhanced by the lack of both piped music and the intrusion of electronic games.

The pub is owned by Shepherd Neame with their Master Brew, Late Red Amber Ale, Spitfire and Porter featuring.

A regularly changing menu emphasises hearty home cooked fare that is served 12 noon till 2pm and 7 pm till 9 pm. Tuesday to Saturday 12 noon till 2.30 pm on Sunday Choices may include ham, duck egg and chips, smoked haddock macaroni, goats cheese crostini and a range of fresh fish dishes such as halibut, grilled plaice and fish pie. Puddings include hot chocolate fondant with white chocolate sorbet. Hog roasts in the splendid garden are a summer attraction.

Opening times are from 12 noon till 3 pm, and from 6 till 11pm, Sundays 12 – 8 pm. Pub closed on Mondays.

Telephone: 01227 751360.

## Walk No. 8

Village signed off the A299, 4 miles west of Whitstable. Postcode: ME13 9HB.

Approx. distance of walk: 3 miles. OS Map No. 149 TR 080/615.

The inn has its own car park.

*A short peaceful walk through Blean Wood up to Holly Hill. Superb open views across the marshes to the Swale and the Isle of Sheppey. Gentle climbing, but the woodland paths can be very muddy and slippery after wet weather.*

1. Cross the road from the pub and follow the lane sign-posted Herne Hill and Boughton. Where the road curves right, bear off left beside a weather boarded cottage onto a way marked bridleway. At a fork of paths on the woodland edge, keep left and soon enter the delightful mainly beech woodland. Remain on the established path, gently climbing uphill to emerge into a farmyard.

2. Follow the track through the farm between barns. Pass through a gate, then almost immediately turn sharp right (good views) through a further gate (blue arrow) to follow a pitted track towards a house. Keep ahead where track enters the drive of the house, pass through a metal gate and remain on the main worn pathway, fringed with rhododendrons, through woodland. Curve left, shortly to follow woodland fringe with fine views across Seasalter, Whitstable and the Isle of Sheppey. At a fork of paths, keep right to a gate and a lane.

3. Turn right down the narrow little used lane to a T-junction and turn right again. Follow the lane for ¼ mile, then bear left through a metal gate (yellow arrow) and pass The Old Gate House. Keep to the metalled farm track, bearing right at a fork and shortly reach a lane. Turn right back to the pub.

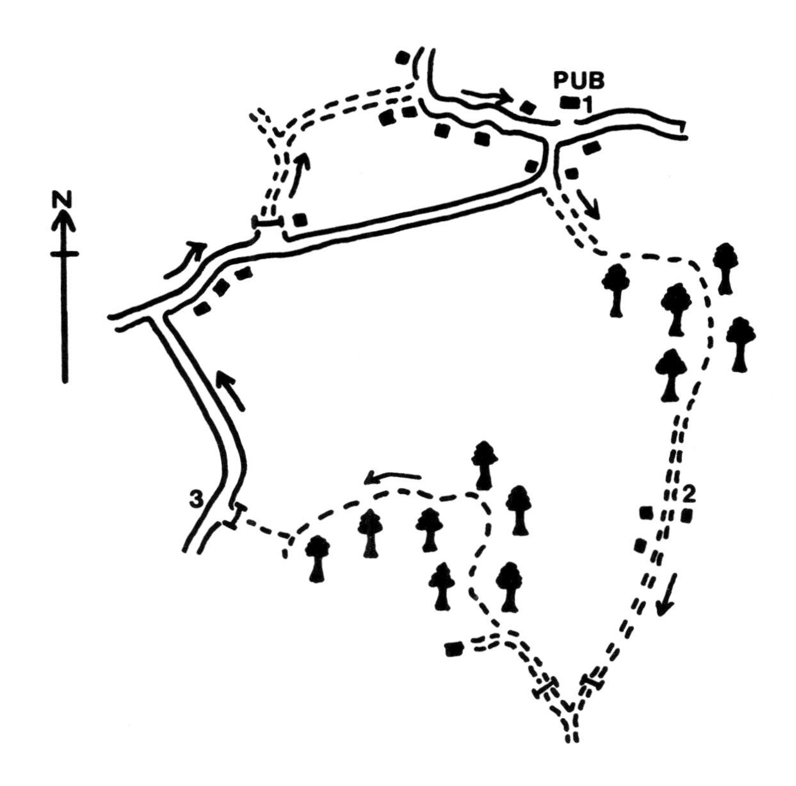

Walk No. 9

# The Carpenters Arms, Eastling

Nestling in a very rural hamlet, the Carpenters Arms dates back to 1380 when it was built as an early Kentish Hall House. It became an ale house quite early on in its history, providing refreshment for the carpenters who worked in the sawmill at the back of the magnificent manor house across the road, which was the birth place of the noted Kentish historian Edward Hasted. The mellow brick façade belies its age hiding the ancient, part-timbered original building which teems with character. The single bar boasts a wealth of beams, a huge brick fireplace with warming log fire and a collection of old furniture, including numerous pews around draw-leaf dining room tables and leather sofas. Plenty of bygones, farming implements, old local photographs and bottles adorn the room while the candle-topped tables enhance the relaxing atmosphere. The separate, cosy low beamed restaurant features a red-brick floor, a vast inglenook with bread oven and lace clothed tables, complete with flowers and candles.

On draught in this Shepherd Neame house are the well kept brewery ales, Master Brew, Spitfire, Original Porter and Mild.

Good home-cooked food is served from 12 noon till 10 pm daily except Sunday when it finishes at 5 pm. The bar menu features sound home-cooked favourites such as steak and kidney pie, lamb casserole, chilli, beef or chicken curry, hearty soups, ham, egg and chips, a range of toasted sandwiches and ploughman's. Daily specials are available and may include potted crab, deep fried pigs cheek and roast red pepper mousse followed by game dishes like pot roasted pheasant in season and roast saddle of hare. At least five tempting puds. Sunday roast.

Opening times Monday to Thursday 12 noon till 3 and 6 till 11 pm, Friday and Saturday 12 noon till Midnight and Sunday 12 noon till 7 pm.

Children are welcome and dogs if on a lead.

Telephone: 01795 890234, thecarpentersarmseastling.co.uk.

**Walk No. 9**

Village is located on a lane 3 miles south west of the A2 at Faversham. Postcode: ME13 0AZ.

Approx. distance of walk: 2½ miles. OS Map No. 149 TQ 963/506.

The pub has its own car park and walkers can use the church car park up the lane.

*A short, delightful rural walk across farmland and through peaceful woodland. Easy going and an ideal family stroll. Eastling church is well worth a visit and the churchyard boasts a fine ancient yew tree. The splendid timbered manor house near the pub is reputed to be the second oldest building in Kent.*

1. From the car park turn left along the village lane, pass the left turning to Newnham, then enter the field on your right (not waymarked) and follow the left-hand edge. Bear right to a stile on your left, keep left-handed, then where the path joins a grassy track to a barn, turn right and keep left of a line of trees. At the end of the trees head diagonally left across the field on a defined path towards a house. On reaching a crossroads of paths by the house, turn right through scrub and across a field to enter woodland.

2. At a crossing of tracks, turn right with blue arrow and follow the wide track through the woodland fringe to a lane. Turn right, then at the beginning of some white railings, bear off left onto a waymarked path uphill into woods. Curve right then left and bear right on a narrow ill-defined path through the trees to a stile on the woodland edge. Continue straight across an open field, then just before reaching the perimeter fence and house, turn right to a stile visible in the hedgerow. Bear right across a paddock to a stile, keep left to a further stile beside house and continue across a field and along the field edge to a waymarked gap (yellow arrow), leading between properties on a drive to a lane. Turn left back to the pub.

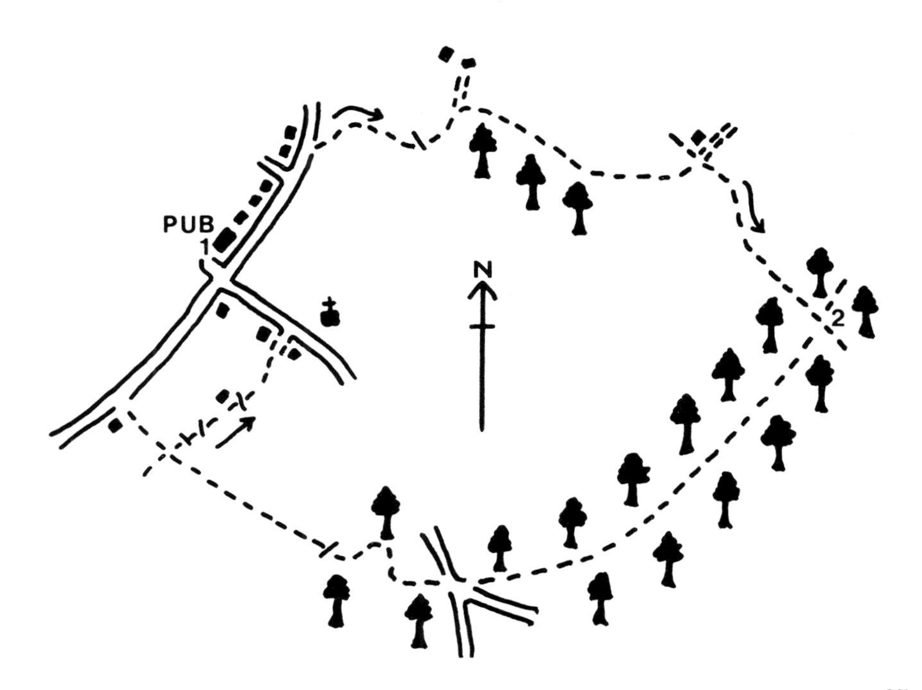

Walk No. 10

# The Fordwich Arms, Fordwich

This solid Tudor-style village pub was built 70 years ago on the site of the ancient long weather-boarded hostelry that was burnt down in 1928. Enjoying a fine setting beside the River Stour, St Mary's church and the tiny half-timbered medieval town hall, it was once a crane-house collecting tolls from goods unloaded at the town quay at the time when the Stour was navigable and Fordwich was Canterbury's port. Civilised alfresco drinking can be savoured on the delightful riverside terrace and garden. The handsome woodblock-floored long bar has open fires at each end, fine arched windows and is smartly furnished with plush seating, some in quiet secluded alcoves. China plates, various pictures and a collection of copper jugs and other bygones decorate the walls. There is also a separate dining room where children are most welcome.

Real ales on draught generally include Flowers Original, Wadsworth 6X, Shepherd Neame Master Brew plus a guest.

Good popular bar food is served daily except Sunday evenings from 12 noon till 2.30 pm, 3 pm on Sundays and 6.30 till 9.30 pm. The interesting snack menu includes an impressive range of 9 types of ploughman's, from local sausage to home-cooked ham, homemade soup of the day, stuffed jacket potatoes, freshly prepared sandwiches, large filled cottage rolls and a choice of salads. Daily hot dishes are listed on a blackboard and may feature filo prawns, grilled goats cheese, braised beef with ale and mushrooms, steak and kidney pie, chicken and apricot curry and Tuscan style lamb and rabbit casserole. There is a vegetarian option, dish of the day and a good selection of puddings and coffees.

Dogs on leads are welcome in the bar and garden.

Telephone: 01227 710444.

Village is signposted off the A28 at Sturry, 2 miles north-east of Canterbury. Postcode: CT2 0DB

Approx. distance of walk: 3½ miles. OS Map No. 150 TR 180/698

There is a small car park at the inn and some space on the village lane.

*A short pleasant walk through the Stour Valley along good woodland and field paths and quiet narrow lanes. The attractive village of Fordwich was once Canterbury's River Stour port and the ancient town hall beside the pub is the smallest in the country and preserves a medieval ducking stool.*

1. From the pub follow the Stour Valley Walk sign left, passing Monks Hall and bear left onto School Lane, a narrow tarmac path between properties. Climb a stile, cross pasture to a further stile, bear left onto a track and follow Stour Valley Walk markers through the edge of a tree plantation to stile proceeding woodland. Gently climb on a defined path through sweet chestnut coppice, then in ½ mile look out for a sign arrowing you right uphill to a stile on the woodland fringe.

2. Keep left-handed, passing Higham Farm (good Stour Valley views) on the left to a stile and turn right up the driveway to a lane. Cross straight over, climb a fence stile beside a gate and proceed on a grassy track to a further gate and enter woodland. At a staggered crossroads of tracks go straight on, pass beside game bird pens, then disregard the track to your left and continue to cross a small stream.

3. Turn immediately left along the field edge to a stile beside a gate onto a lane near Swanton Farm. Turn right and follow the lane for about 400 yards until reaching a gate on your left. Bear off right onto a diagonal grassy path through partially cleared woodland then descend through chestnut coppice into a field. Keep to the right-hand edge, re-enter woodland, cross a small brook and shortly reach a crossing of paths. Turn left (can be muddy) and follow the path as it bears right uphill to a lane beside Trenley Lodge. Turn left then take the narrow lane right and descend into Fordwich. Keep straight ahead on merging with the village lane and turn right at the sharp left-hand bend back to the pub.

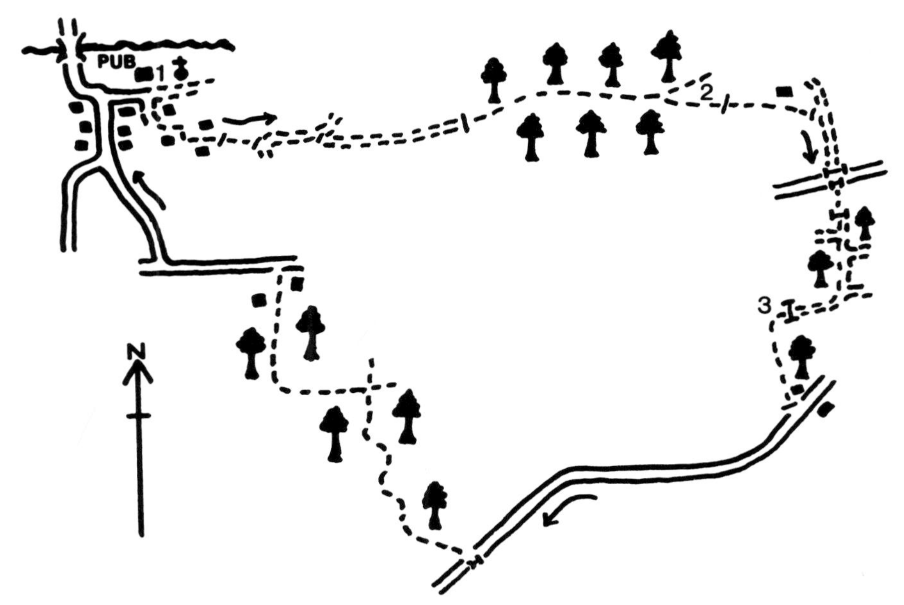

Walk No. 11

# The Star and Eagle, Goudhurst

Dating back to the 14th-century this ancient hostelry commands a lofty position next to the parish church, 400 ft above sea level with outstanding views across the Kentish Weald. Relics of vaulted stonework in some parts of the building suggest that the inn is built on the site of a medieval monastery. More recently in the 18th-century it was used by the infamous 'Hawkhurst Gang', a band of smugglers who robbed and terrorised the area and it is reputed that contraband was stored in a tunnel which linked the inn to the church. The public areas boast a wealth of beams, exposed brickwork and a fine inglenook fireplace. The refectory dining room enjoys some splendid countryside views whilst the character bar welcomes walkers and provides a choice from Harveys Sussex, Adnams Southweld and Westerham Grasshopper.

Food service is 12 noon till 2.30 pm and 7 till 9.30 pm, Sundays 12 till 2.30 and 6.30 till 9 pm. The menu is the sort to tempt you to stay a fortnight. For example, starters such as king prawns sautéed in garlic, chillies, white wine and parsley, large grilled Portuguese sardines or smooth chicken liver, smoked bacon and brandy pate. "Lighter" main meals include spicy meatballs and spaghetti, sausage and mash, ham, egg and chips and lasagne, while vegetarians have a splendid choice from cannelloni pancakes, mushroom crepes, stuffed peppers and curry. It makes one's mouth water just reading the rest of the fish and meat courses not forgetting the puddings – suffice it to say you will find something to delight you.

Opening times are from 11am till 11 pm, Sunday 12 noon till 10.30 pm.

Children are welcome in the dining areas but not the main bar. Dog are welcome on the terrace but not inside the premises.

There are ten individually styled bedrooms.

Telephone: 01580 211512.

Village is located on the A262 between Cranbrook and the A21 north of Lamberhurst. Postcode: TN17 1AL

Approx. Distance of walk: 3¼ miles. OS Map No. 136 TQ 724/378.

The inn has some parking spaces to the front and a rear car park.

*A short farmland walk through the Teise Valley, returning to the attractive hill-top village of Goudhurst via established orchard tracks. Fine rural views, relatively easy and good underfoot make it an ideal walk for the whole family. Further exploration in the area reveals Finchcocks (1½ miles west), a fine Georgian house with an outstanding collection of musical instruments dating from the 17th-century. South of Goudhurst is the magnificent pinetum at Bedgebury.*

1. From the front of the inn turn left down the High Street into the village centre and turn right at the crossroads by the pond. Disregard the first waymarked path left and take the second arrowed route between Chequers garage and an estate agents, signed Trottenden. Shortly climb a stile (good views) and follow the worn path right to cross a stile near a pond. Continue downhill on the defined path through pasture to a further stile and plank footbridge, then keep right on a grassy path to a stile in the field corner. At a grassy track turn right, soon to bear off right across a plank footbridge to a stile.

2. Cross a lane and a further stile and proceed straight ahead, passing between two trees to a stile and a lane. Turn right, then left beyond a pond along the driveway to Trottenden Farm. Bear right with concrete waymarker before the oast houses and follow the drive past a brick and weatherboard house to a stile flanking a gate. Continue along a track, pass through a gate and maintain direction across pasture to a stile. Keep ahead to a further waymarked stile, then follow path into open pasture and bear

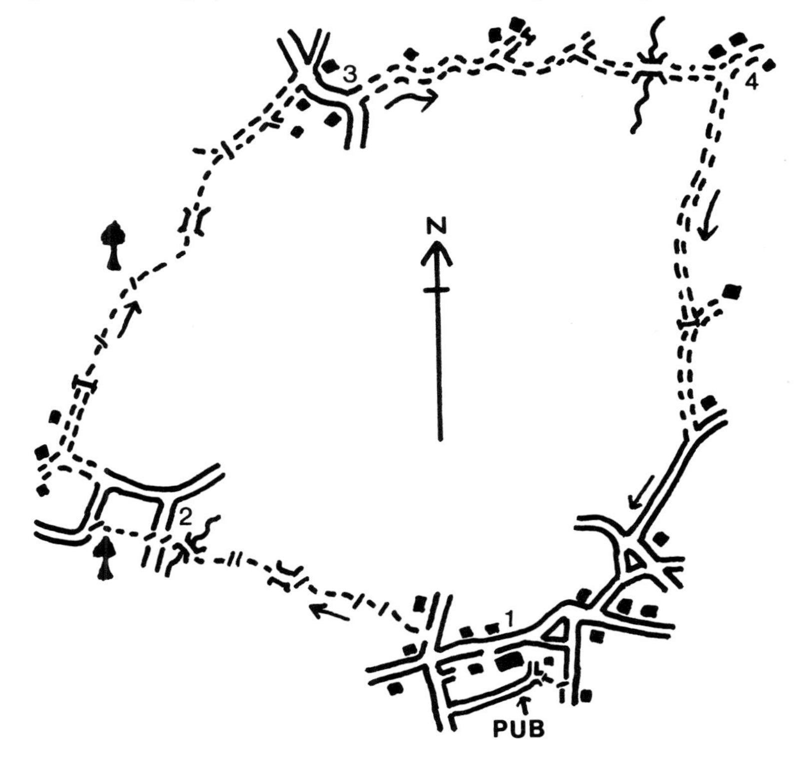

right along the field edge to a footbridge over a brook. Keep right-handed to a stile, then gradually climb uphill on a wide pathway, then driveway to the road.

3. Turn right then at a pink and white cottage cross over to follow a waymarked bridleway. Soon pass Swan Cottage, then just before the gate to the black and white timbered Swan Farm, bear right (yellow arrow) to join a grassy track along the edge of an orchard. Shortly, where the track divides, follow the arrowed route right and remain on the track across a brook, then gradually climb uphill to Bockingfield Farm.

4. At a T-junction of tracks with the farm to your left, turn right gently uphill along an established track. Eventually, pass through a gate and keep right along a driveway to a road. Turn right, shortly to go straight over a crossroads with B-road, then keep right at the next junction to reach the A262. Bear right along the footway, then in a few yards cross over into a lane and keep left down a narrow wooden lane. Just before reaching a house on your left, take the arrowed path right up a steep bank to a stile, then proceed ahead along the field edge to a stile in the corner by a hall. Bear left along drive to a lane opposite Goudhurst church. Turn left back to the rear car park of the inn.

Peaceful parkland views at Godinton near Great Chart

# The Hoodener's Horse, Great Chart

This unassuming, red brick terraced village local was transformed in the 1990's when it became part of a small chain of pubs opened by Alex Bensley, all having the 'Hooden Horse' theme. The name Hooden Horse now changed to Hoodner's Horse. The origins of the pub name are uncertain, but it most probably refers to the threatening prop that was used by labourers at Christmas a few hundred years ago, to collect gifts from people for the poor and needy. The rustic interior comprises a long bar with two small inter-connecting rooms. The ceiling is festooned with hops and the bare boarded and tiled floors are laid out with a simple mix of pub furniture, including wheel back chairs, stools and round tables topped with colourful candles in old wine bottles. Morris dancers are regular visitors.

They have an excellent choice of well kept real ales and ciders including Sharp's Doom Bar and St Austell's Tribute with regularly changing guests.

Renowned for its Mexican food which is available 12 noon till 2.30 pm and 6 till 9.30 pm, Mon-Sun. Devotees come from far and wide to sample their enchiladas, fajitas, tacos, burritos nachos and chilli con carne. Fillings can be vegetarian as required and those preferring normal pub grub will find that they have not been forgotten. English fayre is available in the form of fresh fish in homemade beer batter, salmon and dill fish cakes, chicken and bacon Caesar salad and the Hoodener's burger and chips. Delightful sweets include sticky toffee pudding, spotted dick and syrup sponge.

Opening hours are 11 am till 11 pm, Sunday 12 noon till 10.30 pm

Children and dogs are welcome.

Telephone: 01233 625583. hoodnershorse.co.uk

## Walk No. 12

Village lies just off the A28 Ashford to Tenterden road 2 miles south west of Ashford. Postcode: TN23 3N.

Approx. distance of walk: 4¾ miles. OS Map No. 137 TQ 982/421.

Parking is very limited at the inn, roadside spaces being at a premium.

*This scenic and varied walk through the Great Stour Valley incorporates good tracks and the well waymarked Greensand Way, which traverses both Hothfield and Godinton Parks. The going underfoot can be very wet and muddy in places after rain. Splendid North Downs views.*

1. On leaving the pub turn right along the village street. Pass the parish church and a house on your right, then turn right along a concrete farm driveway and pass Court Lodge Farm. Go through the farmyard and remain on the concrete farm road with good views to the north and follow the grassy track left at its end, soon to pass in front of Godwell Farm. Beyond the garden climb the stile on the right, pass between the house and garage and follow metalled driveway to a lane. Keep straight on across the railway bridge and follow the lane through the hamlet of Worten.

2. Cross the River Stour, then just beyond the Southern Water fenced area, go through a field entrance and follow a narrow worn path across rough pasture and beside fencing to a stile. Climb a further stile and wooden steps up and across an embankment and track to a

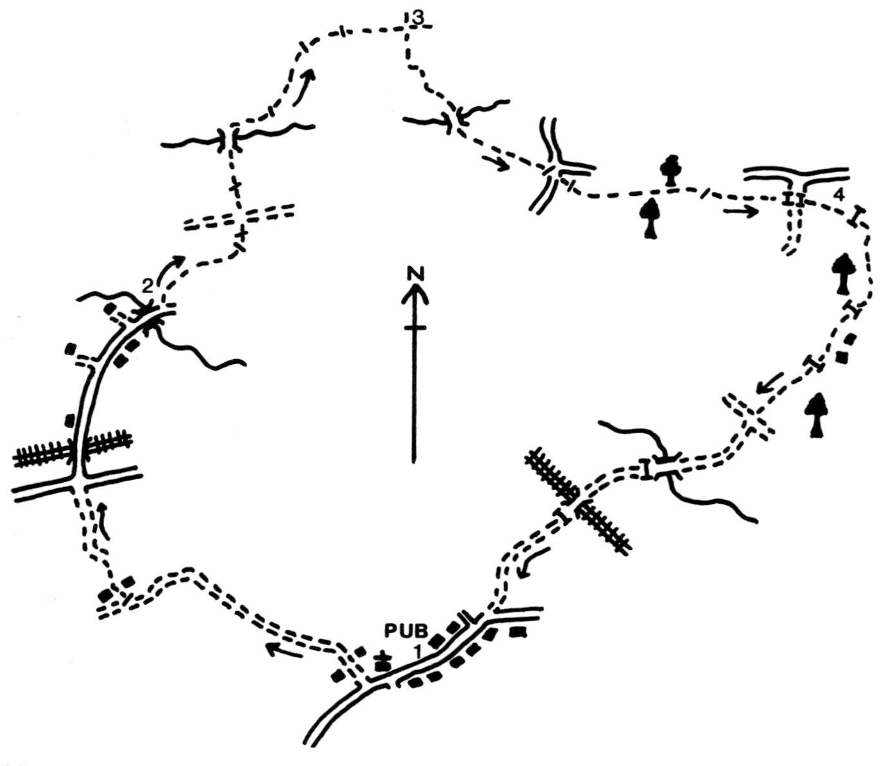

stile. Proceed ahead over what can be quite marshy ground in winter and cross a grassy 'bridge' between water filled dykes. Take the bridge over the stream and beyond the stile bear diagonally left across a field to a stile, then maintain direction across a further field to another stile and head half right to join a track beside some pens.

3. At a stile on your left, turn right onto a grassy path between pens and soon follow yellow arrow and Greensand Way marker half-left across parkland to a footbridge over a stream. Keep ahead beside fencing, then bear diagonally left to a stile in the field corner and a junction of lanes. Cross over with waymarker to a stile beside a pill box, turn left along field edge and shortly follow the path through the coppice, parallel to a lane, to a stile on the woodland fringe. Bear left through the centre of pasture and soon cross the driveway to Godinton House via two metal kissing gates.

4. Proceed ahead to another kissing gate and turn right along field edge, waymarked Great Chart. Keep right with yellow arrow along a field-edge track beside woodland, following it right again between copse to a metal kissing gate. Continue through parkland, then keep straight ahead on reaching a track, soon to cross a stream and railway before joining the lane in Great Chart. Bear right back to the pub.

Church of St. Mary the Virgin and 15th-century timber framed Pest House at Great Chart

**Walk No. 13**

# The Crown Inn, Groombridge

At the end of an attractive row of cottages, this quaint, Elizabethan tile-hung inn overlooks the village green and lies only a stones throw from the Kent/Sussex border. Originally a coaching inn, it is rumoured that it was once a smugglers haunt, with a tunnel running between Groombridge Place and the pub. The sunny front brick terrace is lined with rustic benches and is a delightful place to enjoy a fine weather drink. The interior comprises a series of three relaxing and characterful rooms. A lively local atmosphere fills the main bar which has a copper topped serving counter, a splendid brick inglenook with log fire and original fire irons and spit and heavily beamed ceiling adorned with pewter tankards and jugs. To the left of this bar is a small separate 'snug' room which is ideal for families. Beams and unspoilt charm are maintained in the larger dining area. Pleasant window seats enjoy the lovely village view across the green.

Customers at this busy freehouse can select from ales provided by Harveys, Larkin's and Heyworth's on hand pump. Wine imbibers can choose by the bottle or glass from a good global list.

Tasty home-cooked food is served between 11 am and 3 pm and from 6 till 9.30 pm, Sunday 12 noon till 3.30 pm. Popular bar food dishes include sound pub favourites like sausage and onion pie, steak and kidney pie, fish pie, prawn curry, ploughman's, home-baked ham and chips and sausage and chips, plus good daily specials, for example a hearty soup and winter game pies. Vegetarian choices range from Chinese spring rolls and vegetable curry to a nut roast.

Weekday opening times are from 11 am till 3 pm and 6 pm till 11 pm, Saturday all day 11 pm till 11 pm, Sunday 12 noon till 10.30 pm (5.30 pm in winter).

Children are welcome in the snug bar and restaurant with dogs only in the main bar.

The inn has 4 letting bedrooms.

Telephone: 01892 864742.

Village straddles the Kent/Sussex border on the B2110 between Hartfield and Langton Green, 4 miles south-west of Tunbridge Wells. Postcode: TN3 9QH.

Approx. distance of walk: 3 miles. OS Map No. 135 TQ 530/377.

There is a small car park to the rear of the inn and roadside parking beside the front green.

*A short peaceful walk close to the River Grom which forms the border between Kent and Sussex. The well waymarked field paths can be wet and muddy in winter so waterproof footwear is essential.*

1. From the inn cross the busy B-road, pass through a wooden gate onto a fenced path between a weather boarded cottage and chapel. Beyond a further gate follow the arrowed path across parkland towards Groombridge Place and shortly cross driveway via a gate. Proceed beside the lake, across a bridge, alongside iron fencing and beside the moated house to a gate. Keep ahead, pass through a kissing gate and join a worn path across an open field to a stile. Shortly, cross a waymarked footbridge, then follow a line of pollarded willows, bearing left to a stile and driveway to converted oasts on your left.

2. Cross over (yellow arrow), your path soon becoming hedged as it skirts a sewage works to a stile and lane. Turn right, cross the river, pass beneath the railway bridge and shortly take the arrowed path right to a stile into pasture. Keep right-handed, pass through a gate and bear right onto a metalled driveway, following signs for Crestala. The driveway soon becomes pitted. Then just beyond white cottages on your right, bear right with yellow arrow and keep left of a barn to follow path down a few steps and beside an office to a junction of paths.

3. Proceed ahead on grass centred track, cross a stream, and then bear immediately right with waymarker into a field. Keep to the left-hand edge uphill, then at a fingerpost cross an open field to a bridge over a stream and continue on a worn path to a stile. Follow the line of trees through pasture to a further stile, then in a few yards turn right through a gate and pass beneath the railway to a stile. Keep straight ahead (can be muddy), then cross a stile flanking a gate on your left and continue through parkland towards Groombridge Place. Climb a stile, walk through an avenue of trees, then bear right across a stone bridge and rejoin the outward route back to the inn.

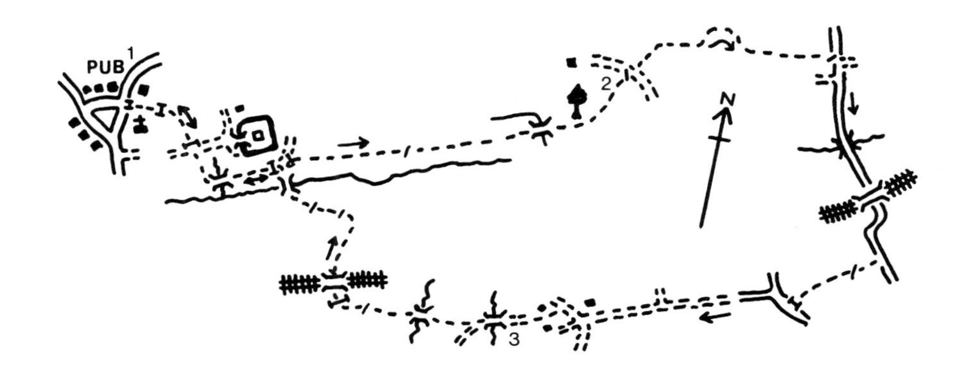


The sketch maps in this book are not necessarily to scale but have been drawn to show maximum amount of detail.

**Walk No. 14**

# The Harrow, Hadlow

There are many main road pubs that seem to attract the worst kind of passing trade, but not the smart Harrow. A place for discerning locals that visitors would be fortunate to find. There is a comfortable bar and prettily decorated conservatory which has a fireplace and candlelit tables most of which are set up for couples which is indicative of the cosy atmosphere. Outside there is a grassy garden with benches and a well equipped play area with slide and climbing frame. The staff are certainly welcoming and helpful and we were easily persuaded to return in the evening.

Owned by Shepherd Neame offering a selection of their real ales; presently Spitfire and Master Brew with Late Red in season.

The extensive, menu available 12 noon till 3 pm and 6 till 9 pm, Sunday 12 till 4 pm, is all cooked to order and that patience is a virtue. Sandwiches are made with white or granary bloomers and served with crisps and salad garnish. Starters include homemade soup of the day, seafood platter, confit duck leg and king prawns with a Thai green curry sauce. Main courses have a good choice of ploughman's and salads, steak and kidney pudding, ham, egg and chips, sirloin steak and homemade 'Harrow Burger'. If you fancy more exotic fare there is pan fired black bream on fennel, breast of chicken in sherry sauce, haunch of venison and smoked haddock gratin. For vegetarians, what about Portobello mushrooms filled with Stilton and topped with a Parmesan and herb crust. The puddings are all homemade. Children have their own menu.

Well behaved dogs on leads.

Opening times 12 noon till 11 pm, Sunday 12 noon till 6 pm.

Telephone: 01732 850386.

## Walk No. 14

The pub is located on the A26 Maidstone Road at Hadlow. Postcode: TN11 0HP.

Approx. distance of walk: 4¼ miles. OS Map No. 148 TQ 637/504

There is a good sized car park at the rear.

*A breezy stroll across the expanse of Oxen Hoath Park, then a visit to lovely West Peckham and a sighting of a novel bird scarer on the return across farmland.*

1. Turn left out of the pub and at Jasmine Cottage cross the road to a kissing gate to a signed path. At the end bear left into a field then right again to follow the field edge to a metal gate and path. At a lane turn left then right into Carpenter's Lane and, at the junction with Common Lane, cross to a kissing gate and go ahead up a field on a grass path. At the next kissing gate maintain direction through Oxen Hoath Park, soon with a wire fence to your right. After another kissing gate the path starts to bend right. Pass through the pillared gateway with Oxen Hoath over to your right.

2. You exit between more pillars and take the central path of three before you. At a fork keep ahead right and at a T-junction turn right on a track. We saw a muntjac deer here in the young orchard on the right. Join the Greensand Way and at a road turn left where, in a few yards, the path is signed on the right. A gate leads into a field, keep along the left-hand side and out through a gate to a bungalow. To the left you can see West Peckham's church and you head along the track and across the village green to the immaculate church of St Dunstan's. Its origins are Saxon although it is mostly Norman. In an idyllic setting by the green and a pub with its own microbrewery you may be tempted to linger.

3. Retrace your steps to the bungalow and turn left down a track. In front of a field opening turn right with a hedge on your left. Pass a large wooden shack and follow the field edge round to a waymarked gate. Turn right on the footpath (ignore signed bridleway going left). Cross a bridge into a field and keep along the field edge past Vines Farm with its novel rooftop bird scarer. Turn left on the road and in 250 yards turn right on a signed track. Pass two houses and where the track bends sharp right to Cricketers Farm go ahead on a grass track. Pass a cricket pitch and continue on a fenced path. At a road turn left and in 200 yards turn right on a signed path. Reach the A26 and turn right back to the pub.

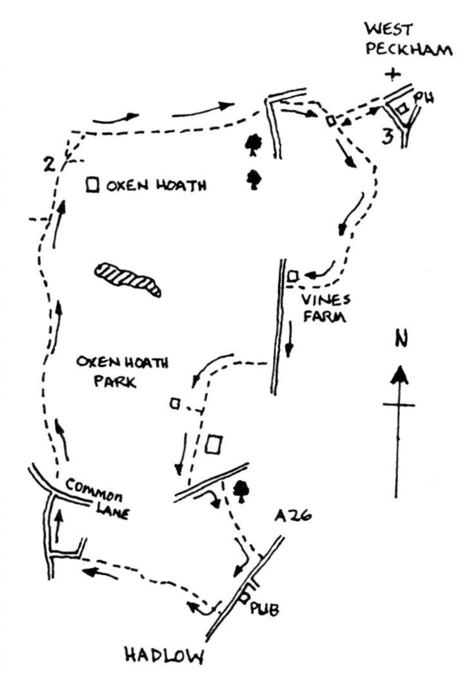

**Walk No. 15**

# The Cock Inn, Henley Street, Luddesdown

The Cock Inn is a traditional pub in every sense of the word and a mecca for real ale enthusiasts. Located in the picturesque Luddesdown Valley on a country lane in a tiny hamlet, it has been a pub since 1713 and prior to this the building was believed to have been a farmhouse. The two unpretentious bars are welcoming and free from music and game machines. The simply furnished public bar has a wood burner, a bar billiards table, a few local prints and a collection of Dinky toys. The comfortable lounge bar has a splendid warming log fire and wall bench seating set within the large bay windows.

It has been under the same management ownership for the past 26 years and in 2010, this classic unassuming pub was described by CAMRA as 'a shining example of how a good pub should be run'. The choice of 7 real ales can include Whistable E.I.P.A, Adnams Bitter and Broadside plus guests from regional and micro breweries and there is always a mild available.

This traditional ambience and atmosphere of a pub in bygone days is maintained in the limited and simple yet hearty bar snacks and basket meals. Available from 12 noon till 9 pm they consist of a wide range of filled submarine rolls, bruschettas and French bread pizzas. In addition in winter there will be beef lasagne, lamb shank cooked in red wine, a vegetarian risotto and a bowl of hot soup with bread and at weekends during the summer a variety of barbecue dishes which can be enjoyed on the terrace. Although only serving simple food they were recently voted by the Times newspaper as one of the best 50 places to eat in the countryside. Of interest to smokers there is a fully under cover heated area in the rear garden.

This is an adults only pub and no one under the age of 18 is permitted inside.

Opening times every day 12 noon till 11 pm.

Telephone: 01474 814208.

Henley is signposted from Sole Street, off the lane between Cobham and Meopham near Gravesend. Postcode: DA13 0XB.

Approx. distance of walk: 5 miles. OS Map No. 148 TQ 664/672.

The inn has a large car park.

*An undulating and varied walk along field paths, across farmland and pastures and through peaceful woodland on wide, muddy tracks. Well waymarked, easy to follow and very scenic. Owletts (NT) at Cobham, a fine red-brick Charles II house is worth a visit (open April to September, Wednesday and Thursday only).*

1. From the pub turn right along the lane, pass the Old Post Office and turn right over a stile (path 188), waymarked, Luddesdown Church. Head uphill on a defined path, cross stile, pass through a narrow thicket and continue across an open field on a worn path towards the church to a lane. Cross over onto a tarmac track, signed to the church, then just before large wooden gates and barn, turn left onto an arrowed path (214) down to a stile. Keep ahead along the field edge to a stile and climb uphill between trees to an open field and a junction of paths. Turn right and follow the field edge to a lane.

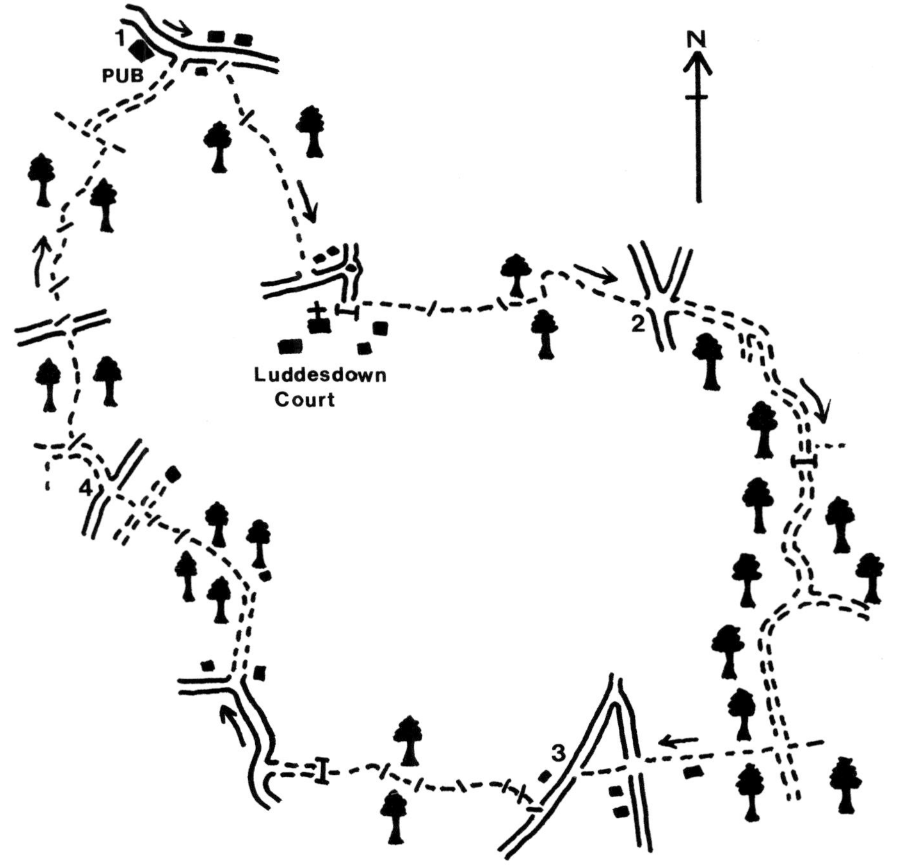

2. Cross onto a waymarked track and continue climbing through the woodland. Follow yellow arrows, remain on the main track at the top, then at the arrowed gatepost and junction of paths proceed with yellow arrow along the muddy track. At a fork, keep right, then bear left just before two pylons and follow the track through the woodland fringe to an arrowed post. Turn right onto a narrow path downhill past a cottage to a lane. Turn left, then immediately right onto the path beside 'Thatched Cottage' to a further lane.

3. Turn left, pass Great Buckland Farm and cross a stile on the right into pasture. Follow yellow waymarkers across stiles and pastures uphill to a stile preceding woodland. Climb steeply up a stepped path to a stile, then bear slightly left across a paddock and go through a gate, shortly reaching a lane. Turn right, then where the lane bears left beside a black and white timbered cottage, continue ahead along a tarmac drive between the cottage and a barn. Tarmac soon gives way to grass, enter woodland and descend on a well waymarked path to a stile. Proceed ahead across pasture to a stile and cross a driveway onto a narrow, steep pathway to a lane.

4. Cross the lane onto a waymarked fenced bridleway, head uphill and shortly climb the stile on your right into an open field. Keep straight ahead on a worn path, descend and pass through a scrub hedge on the field edge and proceed through the next field to a lane. Cross the stile opposite, waymarked Sole Street and Henley Street, keep left-handed to a further stile, then bear half right to a stile on the woodland edge. Pass through the wood, then follow a grassy path on the field edge to a T-junction of paths. Turn left, then immediately right onto a defined path and gently descend to the lane in Henley Street. Turn left back to the pub.

Woodland track near Luddesdown

**Walk No. 16**

# The Green Man, Hodsoll Street

This delightful white painted cottage nestles beside a small green on a dead-end lane in a tiny rural hamlet. In summer months its façade is ablaze with an award winning floral display of colourful hanging baskets, tubs and window boxes. The name Green Man dates back to 1775-85 when it was given to the leaf clad Mummer. He was generally a chimney sweep who walked encased in a framework of wood or wickerwork which was covered with leaves and occasionally flowers and ribbons. He would dance on May Day and other pageants at the head of the procession to clear the way.

The interior comprises four neatly furnished interconnecting rooms which are warmed by a wood burner and a further open fire in the winter months. Floral wallpaper, old prints and a collection of horse brasses enhance the relaxing, cottagey ambience that prevails throughout the rooms. Fine weather imbibing can be savoured in the peaceful rear garden, complete with picnic benches and children's play area.

Real ales on draught are Timothy Taylor Landlord, Old Speckled Hen and Harvey's Sussex plus usually a guest ale from a local brewery.

This is a popular venue for food with an extensive menu prepared to order from fresh ingredients. Served weekdays 12 noon till 2 pm (Sat 3 pm) and 6.30 till 9.30 pm (Sat 9 pm) Sunday 12 noon till 8.30 pm, they boast that there is something to suit all tastes. Additional blackboard specials may include beef stroganoff, chicken and broccoli in pepper sauce, chicken korma, liver and bacon and a vegetarian lasagne.

Opening times are 11 am till 11 pm, Sunday 12 noon till 10.30 pm.

Both children and dogs are welcome in the bars.

Telephone: 01732 823575.

## Walk No. 16

Hamlet and pub signposted from the A27 between Meopham and Wrotham. Postcode: TN15 7LE.

Approx. distance of walk: 4 miles. OS Map No. 148 TO 625/630.

The inn has its own car park.

*A very rural walk that undulates on well signed paths through woods, across farmland and along short stretches of quiet country lanes. The peacefully located village of Stansted is picturesque with an interesting church.*

1. Leave the pub, turn right past Hodsoll House and the village hall to a T-junction. Turn left and shortly bear off right onto a waymarked by-way past Home Farmhouse. Follow the hedged track to metal gates, enter a farmyard, turn left, pass through a gate onto a track and shortly turn right with yellow arrow (footpath 254/255) onto an established hedged track. Soon follow a field hedge (ignoring path right), enter woodland on path 254, then at the woodland fringe bear left onto path 204 to a stile. Cross two fields via stiles, then bear half-left to a gate and pass a pond to a lane in the hamlet of Fairseat.

2. Cross over onto waymarked path along a drive beside the chapel and Court House Farm. Proceed to a metal gate at the edge of the concrete farmyard, then beyond the fenced grassy track turn right along the field edge to a stile by a water trough across a field corner. Continue ahead downhill, cross a stile by a field entrance and proceed on a worn path to climb two stiles on the field edge. Bear slightly left uphill, follow path through woodland keeping right at the wire fence and follow yellow markers to a stile. Keep to the path, close to woodland fringe and shortly join a good grassy path. Soon bear right across the grassy valley to a stile, head diagonally right uphill to stile by a telegraph pole, and bear half-right to a stile to the right of the house.

3. Keep straight ahead across pasture, climb the stile on your right and follow a tree-lined path gently downhill to a stile. Continue to a stile on the woodland edge, bear right steeply downhill to a further stile and proceed half right on a well marked path across an open field to a stile. Climb through scrub to a stile, keep left to another stile onto a path leading to a lane. Turn right downhill into Stansted, turning right at the T-junction down Plaxdale Green Road to the War Memorial.

4. Keep left, cross Malthouse Road and a waymarked stile and bear diagonally right, steeply uphill to a stile. Turn left onto a stony track, then head half-right across a large open field on a path marked by white painted steaks to a stile and cross a lane. Maintain direction across a further field, pass through a waymarked gateway, then at an arrowed post turn left and bear diagonally right on yellow waymarked path 251. Pass through a gateway and eventually reach a lane beside the driveway to Pettings Farm. Turn right into Hodsoll Street, turning left back along the lane to the pub.

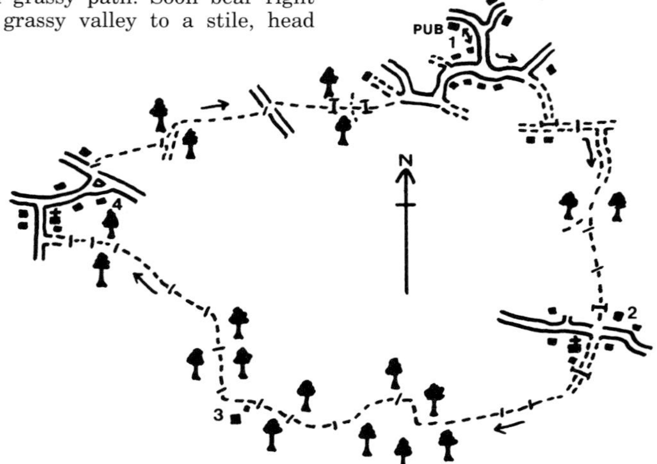

# The Elephant's Head, Hook Green

This fine ancient half-timbered and half-sandstone building enjoys an isolated rural setting overlooking a green, close to Bayham Abbey and the Sussex border. Built as a farmhouse for the Abbey in 1489, it began brewing ales for the estate workers in 1768 and was known as the Elephant Ale House in 1795, acquiring its present name and full licence in 1808. Inside, there is one rambling, opened up bar Elephant-Bar – which retains much of its character and antiquity with front mullioned windows, part brick and part bare wooden floors, stone walls and a heavily beamed ceiling. One corner boasts a huge inglenook fireplace with crackling winter log fires in its unusual raised hearth. A variety of dark wood pub tables and cushioned old church pews furnish the main bar area and the cosy adjacent side rooms. French windows lead out onto a paved terrace and bench filled lawn which look out across peaceful countryside.

It is one of the few pubs to stock the entire range of Harveys ales, namely their Best Bitter, Pale Ale, Armada Ale, XX Mild, and the malty Old Ale.

A regularly changing blackboard menu, served daily 12 noon till 2.30 pm and 7 till 9.30 pm, on my visit included lamb kebabs with rice, cottage pie, sweet and sour pork, steak and kidney pie, tortellini pasta and Bolognese, mixed grill, sausage casserole in a giant Yorkshire pudding, hot roast beef sandwiches, chilli and lasagne. A good vegetarian choice may include a couple of freshly prepared soups – cauliflower/vegetable - spicy bean burgers, cheesy pasta bake and mushroom stroganoff. Sandwiches and ploughman's are always available plus a Sunday carvery. Sunny summer days will see an outdoor barbecue, salad bar and afternoon cream teas.

Weekday opening times are from 12 noon till 3 pm and from 4.30 till 11 pm. Weekends open all day from noon.

Children are made very welcome and dogs allowed in the bar and garden.

Telephone: 01829 890279.

## Walk No. 17

The pub is located beside the B2169 between Lamberhurst and Tunbridge Wells, 2 miles west of Lamberhurst. Postcode: TN3 8LJ.

Approx. distance of walk: 2¾ miles. OS Map No. 136 TQ 655/359.

The pub has car parks to the side and rear, plus space at the front.

*A most enjoyable short rural ramble along undulating field paths and farm tracks, close to the Kent/Sussex border. Nearby attractions include Scotney Castle (NT, open April to early November). Owl House Garden (open daily), and the 13th-century ruins of Bayham Abbey, the old church, cloisters and gatehouse being picturesquely set in the wooded Teise Valley (open daily April to September).*

1. Walk along the metalled slip-road in front of the inn and turn left at the crossroads into Free Heath Lane. Follow the lane for about 200 yards and take the waymarked path left along the driveway to a pair of white cottages. Keep left of the garage, into a field and follow the left-hand edge, shortly to bear off left across a stream into a further field. Maintain course gently uphill, curve right with the field edge, and soon turn left with yellow marker across ditch into a hop field. Keep left-handed, cross a trackway and continue to a lane.

2. Climb the stile opposite, descend and cross a brook, then climb to a further stile and proceed on defined arrowed path to a stile and T-junction of paths. Turn left along a narrow path beside holly hedge to a fence stile and keep left-handed across two fields via a gate to cross a track via two stiles. Continue on narrow path beside wire fence, lakes to the right, and cross two more stiles before bearing right down to a stile and footbridge. Proceed through the woodland, cross a further footbridge, then climb uphill to a stile and keep right-handed along the field edge to a stile and B-road, opposite Furnace Farm.

3. Turn left, then in a little way cross over to pass through a waymarked gate to join a concrete farm track between barns and head downhill to cross a bridge over the River Teise. Keep left along a track, then just beyond a corrugated shed turn left with waymarker into a field and follow the grassy path along the field edge. Shortly, bear off right with the path, cross a stile in front of Furnace Mill. Bear left onto the driveway and turn immediately right onto a narrow path beside the mill and enter the orchard. In the field corner bear right, then left into a hop field. Keep right-handed, then on entering an open field bear slightly left on a worn path and eventually reach the B-road. Turn right back to the pub.

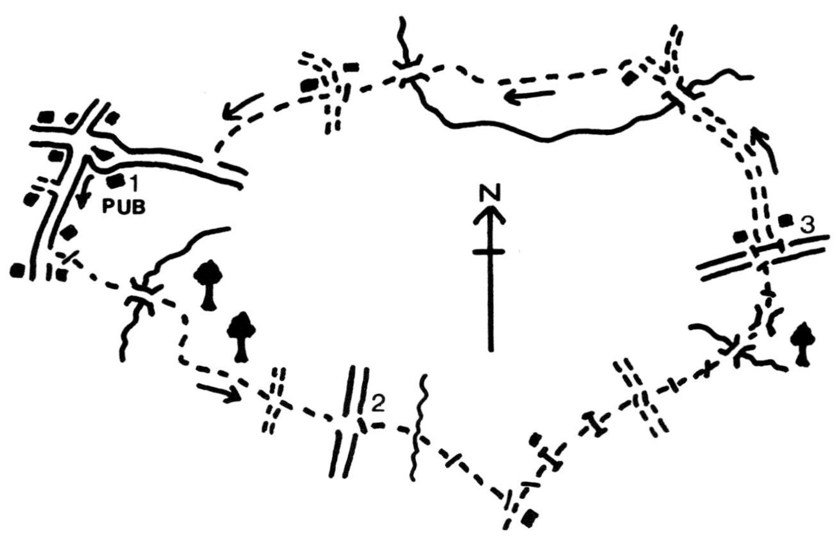

# The Duke William Inn, Ickham

Overlooking the main street in this most peaceful and attractive village are the etched-glass windows of the Duke William, which gives this welcoming 17th-century inn a 19th-century feel. Summer visitors will find this unassuming façade festooned with colourful and overflowing hanging baskets. Originally built as an estate dwelling it became a pub in 1804 when it was taken over by a brewer. The single cosy bar has half panelled walls, a few exposed beams and a large brick fireplace with a log fire all year round. Beyond the bar is a comfortably furnished dining room and a conservatory that leads out to a patio and garden.

This is a freehouse which offers Shepherd Neame Master Brew, Harveys Best and regularly changing guest ales along with a carefully selected wine list.

Food is served 12 noon till 3 pm and 6 till 9.30 pm, Sunday 12 noon till 8 pm. The menu is on a blackboard above the fireplace. Starters include soup, sizzling prawns, scallops and chorizo and field mushrooms with goat's cheese. Main courses start with the 'renowned' steak and ale pie, fresh fish, sirloin steak and local game in season. There is a vegetarian option and the staff will make every effort to meet special requests.

Opening times are 11 am till 11.30 pm (Sunday 11 pm)

Children are welcome and there is a children's menu and play area. Dogs on leads are welcome in the bar.

Four comfortable en-suite bedrooms are available.

Telephone: 01227 721308/721244.

**Walk No.**

Village is signposted off the A257 at Littlebourne, 5½ miles east of Canterbury. Postcode: CT3 1QP.

Approx. distance of walk: 5 miles. OS Map No. 150 TR 220/581.

Parking spaces opposite and along the village lane.

*An enjoyable gentle walk along the Little Stour Valley using a variety of pasture, woodland and farmland paths. Of interest on the walk is Howletts Zoo Park (open daily all year) and nearby is Stodmarsh National Nature Reserve, a haven for migratory and other unusual birds.*

1. From the pub turn right towards the church and turn right just past Dove Cottage onto a narrow waymarked path. At an open field, turn right along the field edge, bearing left past a large shed onto a wide grass-centred track. Soon join a concrete driveway and follow it to the A257. Cross over to a stile onto path CB149, bear slightly right through pasture to another stile and continue beneath two trees to a further stile. Proceed ahead across a lawn in front of house to metalled driveway. Bear left with waymarker over the drive and head across an open field towards the telegraph pole. Pass to its left and continue to a stile. Keep right-handed through pasture to a gate and bear left onto a metalled driveway.

2. At a sharp left bend, proceed straight ahead onto a gravel track, which soon becomes grassy, passing brick cottages to a gate. Cross a track and follow the grassy path along the base of a hill to a stile. Continue to another stile, then drop down to follow the course/channel of the Nail Bourne (can be dry) and soon pass to the right of a fence. Proceed beside the channel to a kissing gate and a tunnel under the railway. Keep left over the river channel to a further kissing gate and bear diagonally left across pasture to a stile. Keep ahead between apple trees to a tall popular hedge. Turn left, then shortly right through a gap in the hedge and head diagonally left between lines of apple trees to a gateway near the white Woolton Farm sign and a lane. Turn right if you wish to visit Howletts Zoo.

3. Turn left along the lane, then at a house on your left, climb the stile opposite (can be overgrown) and keep left-handed along the field edge to a stile. Proceed between wire fence and a tall hedge between orchards to a further stile. Keep ahead alongside fence and soon climb stile beside a gate on your right. Keep left, climb a further stile and soon turn left into a farm complex. Bear left beside large green sheds, then turn right between

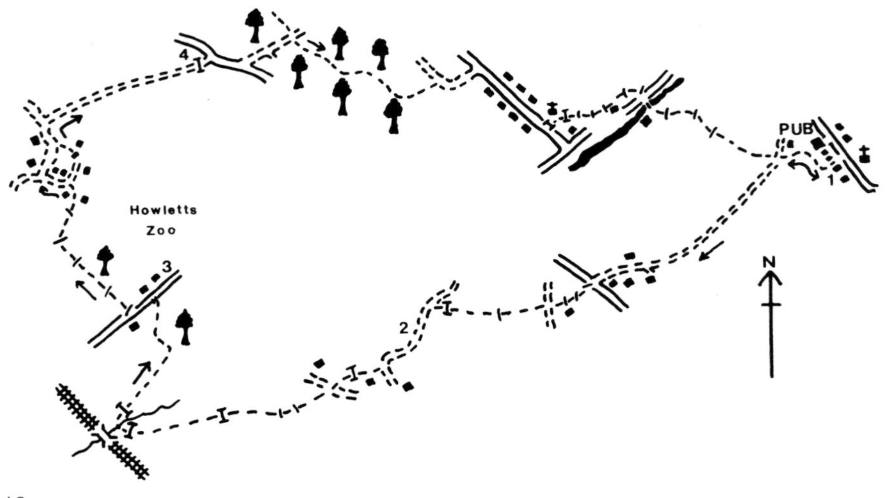

farm buildings along path arrowed to the A257. Keep left at a thatched barn, then bear right at a fork to follow metalled driveway to the main road.

4. Turn right, cross over onto the footway and soon turn left onto a woodland track. Take the second pathway on your right and follow it through woodland to a metalled farm track. Bear right, keep right on merging with a lane and head downhill into Littlebourne. Enter the churchyard on your left, follow the path to the right of the church to a kissing gate and cross a stile to your left. Keep right-handed on a defined path and cross a series of stiles, eventually reaching a lane beside a weather boarded mill. Walk along a grass verge, cross the road and the driveway of a mill to a stile. Keep right to a further stile, cross pasture to a footbridge, then follow worn path to another stile. Cross an open field towards a metal barn and rejoin outward route back into Ickham.

Weatherboarded Littlebourne Mill and The Little Stour river

**Walk No. 19**

# The Plough, Ivy Hatch

The Plough is nestled in the picturesque village of Ivy Hatch just a short walk from the Ightham Mote, Britain's best preserved medieval house. The Plough itself is 230 years old and has a bar area, conservatory and small private dining room all of which were renovated in 2010 by new owners. There is a dining terrace to the front of the building and gardens to the rear surrounded by the local cobnut trees.

The inn is a free house and the management's aim is to bring The Plough back into being the centre of the community whether it be drinks for weary workers or full meals for hungry families, all are catered for.

Beers are from Harveys and Westerham breweries, juices from local producers Owletts Farm, cider from Weston's Stowford Press, The wine list is extensive and from both new and old world countries

Food service is weekdays 12 noon till 2.45 pm and 6 till 9 pm, Saturdays 12 noon till 3 pm (sandwiches available from 3 – 6 pm) and 6 till 9.45pm. Sundays 12 noon till 6 pm. The British and European influenced menu offers a selection of dishes to suit all tastes and pocket sizes. The policy is "to source the best locally produced farm produce and deliver them into classic dishes". The menu is updated daily with new seasonal ingredients arriving each week, all food created on site with no frozen or brought in dishes. Pub snacks include honey roast ham, chips and egg, venison liver and bacon with mashed potato, shallots and gravy, a smoked chicken Caesar salad with baby gem, anchovies, parmesan and croutons and pomegranate, crumbled goats cheese, rocket and fresh herbs. Restaurant starters range from leek and potato soup with crispy leeks and bread or a warm salad of foie gras, black pudding, poached egg and curly endive. Interesting mains include braised oxtail and root vegetables with confit garlic mash and red kale and baked smoked haddock with new potatoes, spinach, whole grain mustard sauce and poached egg. Children can choose smaller portions from the main menu.

Opening times are weekdays 12 noon till 3 pm and 6 till 11 pm, Saturdays 10 am till 11 pm, Sundays 10 am till 6 pm (May – Sep 10.30 pm).

Dogs are welcome in the garden but not in the premises.

Telephone: 01732 810100.

## Walk No. 19

Village is signposted off the A227 Tonbridge to Borough Green road, 1 mile north of Shipbourne. Postcode: TN15 0NL.

Approx. distance of walk: 4½ miles. OS Map No. 147 TQ 588/545.

Parking is available at both the rear and front of the inn.

*A pleasant undulating ramble along the edge of Ightham Common. With far-reaching cameo views and passing through orchards, woodland and farmland on established tracks. An interesting diversion is to visit Ightham Mote (NT open April to October), a magnificent medieval manor which the walk passes. Knole House and Park (NT – open April to October) is also nearby.*

1. Leave the pub, turn right along the lane and shortly turn left at a fork into Stone Street Road. After about 200 yards turn right into Pine Tree Lane, then turn left onto a waymarked path between Beaconswood and Brackenwood properties. Gradually climb this delightful sunken sandy path along the edge of Ightham Common onto Raspit Hill. Remain on this established path (can be muddy) through trees with cameo views and eventually reach a lane.

2. keep right, pass Seal Primary School and St Lawrence's Church, then where the lane curves right, bear off left onto an arrowed bridleway into woodland. Almost immediately turn left beside a concrete path marker and join a narrow path that leads diagonally left down the wooded hillside to a stile behind a house. Follow the fenced pathway to a further stile and bear left onto a driveway to a lane. Turn right and soon turn left onto a way marked un-metalled bridleway opposite the Padwell Arms pub.

3. Remain on the wide track along the edge of an orchard, keeping left of cottages and eventually reach a lane. Cross straight over onto a waymarked metalled drive, pass a farm on the right, then at a fork of tracks proceed ahead onto an earth track through orchards (yellow markers). The track narrows to a path at the orchard edge and descends through Broadhoath Wood. Your path soon curves left and widens, passing between woodland and farmland to a lane.

4. Turn right soon to experience a fine view of Ightham Mote to your left and shortly pass the entrance to Mote Farm. Almost immediately turn left through a small gate beside the main gates to Ightham Mote and follow the metalled drive right passing the splendid manor. Pass the bottom of the car park, onto a grassy track way, then just beyond the National Trust sign, turn left through a small wooden gate, waymarked with a blue arrow. Gradually climb uphill along the left-hand edge of a field, go through a gateway and follow the defined path through woodland to a wooden gate and junction with the main road. Turn left along a narrow path parallel with the lane and eventually merge with the lane, following it back to the pub.

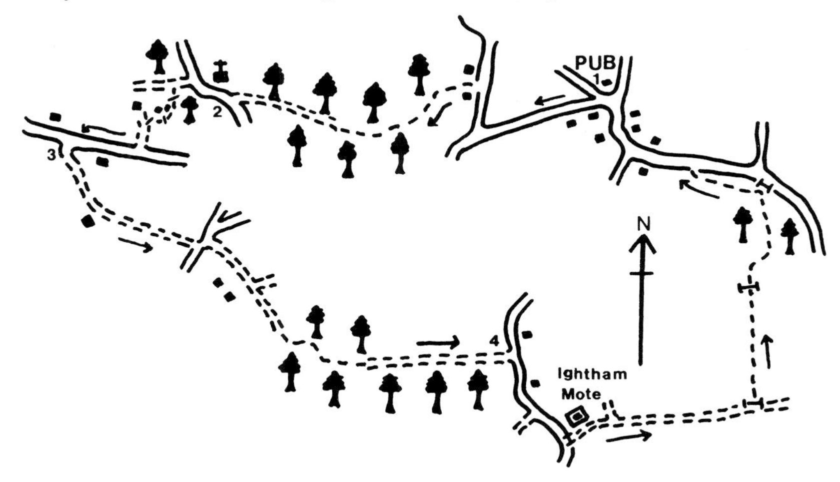

**Walk No. 20**

# The Brown Trout, Lamberhurst

Set back from the road close to the entrance to Scotney Castle (NT), this pretty whitewashed cottage sports brightly coloured hanging baskets and window boxes in the summer months and is especially popular at weekends with visitors seeking out a table and the good selection of food. The pub used to be called The Rising Sun until 1980, when it acquired its present name after a nearby trout reservoir.

The bar has three inter-connecting areas, all beamed, carpeted and comfortably furnished with dark wood tables and chairs. An open basket log fire gives a warm snug feel to the main bar area. Busy summer days see seating overflowing into the picnic bench filled front lawn and into the large secluded rear garden, complete with children's play area.

The pub offers Harveys and Finchcocks ales on hand pump and a good wine list which includes some from the Lamberhurst vineyard along the road.

The food deserves its good reputation and is sourced locally and prepared in modern kitchens. Chutneys, sauces, pates and puddings all home made. Served lunchtimes only in the week from 12 noon till 3 pm, Saturday all day and Sundays 12 noon till 4 and 6 till 9 pm. The menus are augmented by daily specials and a Sunday carvery. If you just want a snack there is a choice of ten fillings to be had in either sandwiches, baguettes or jackets from brie, bacon and chutney to firecracker sausages and sliced peppers. Also ploughman's, homemade burgers, sausage and mash and a vegetarian option. In the restaurant you could start with pan fried butterfly sardines, oven baked mushroom and Stilton bake followed by oven baked lamb cutlets wrapped in a garlic crumb, grilled fillet of red snapper and for vegetarians - homemade mushroom, spinach and roasted pepper lasagne.

Opening times 12 noon till 11 pm, (Saturday 11 am).

Children welcome, dogs also on leads inside and out.

Telephone: 01892 890755.

The pub is located at The Down on the B2169 Frant road, just off the A21 south of Lamberhust near the entrance to Scotney Castle. Postcode: TN3 8HA.

Approx. distance of walk: 4¾ miles. OS Map No. 136 TQ 675/355.

Limited parking beside the inn, but there is a free public car park a few yards along the lane.

*A splendid gently undulating walk through the National Trust parkland of Scotney Castle – the old remains and the beautiful gardens are well worth a visit in the Teise Valley. Also of interest are the 13 acres of romantic gardens (open daily) belonging to Owl House, a small timber framed 16th-century house located a mile west of Lamberhurst. Wine lovers will appreciate a visit to the village's successful vineyard. A peaceful, scenic and easy going walk.*

1. From the pub turn right along the B-road, then on reaching the A21, cross over to follow the waymarked path along the metalled driveway to Scotney Castle (NT). Pass a lake and take the arrowed path right – Kilndown – to a gate. Proceed straight ahead downhill through parkland to a bridge and gate. Continue over a further bridge, go through a gate and gradually climb on defined track to gate preceding woodland.

2. On reaching a junction of tracks, turn left with waymarker and remain on the track uphill through woodland, ignoring turnings left and right. At the top of the rise where the track curves right, keep ahead on the pathway, shortly to pass a cottage on your left. Continue into the village of Kilndown. Turn left along the road, disregard two arrowed paths left, then bear left along the waymarked gravel drive towards Hillside Cottage. Pass to its left, then at a fingerpost turn left up steps to a stile. Proceed straight across pasture soon to follow field edge (waymarker) to a stile in the corner. Cross a further stile, turn immediately right along the field edge to a gate and follow a good path through woodland to a stile flanking a gate.

3. Bear slightly left on a worn path downhill across a field towards oasts to a stile and farmland, then turn left across a bridge and climb the arrowed stile on your right. Cross pasture to a stile, then bear half-left to a gate. Turn left along a grassy path below a bank and proceed to a gate, then either head

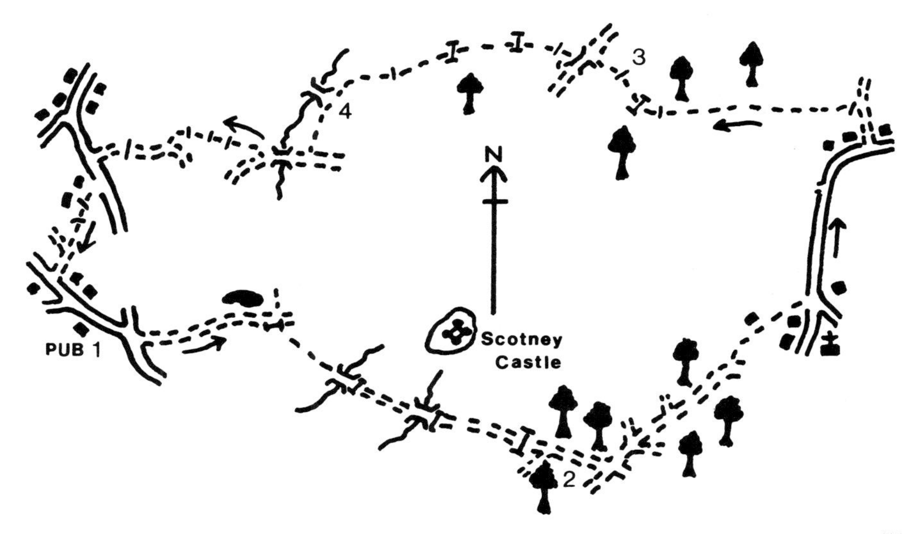

straight across the open field, or follow the field edge left-handed to a waymarked stile in the hedgerow opposite. Maintain direction on the well worn path through an open field and soon follow the right-hand edge, parallel to the River Teise.

4. Keep to the field edge, disregard two footbridges right and continue to a concrete farm track. Turn right over a bridge and bear diagonally right on a worn path to a stile onto the golf course. Proceed ahead, cross two stiles, then bear left around the edge of a playing field, soon to bear left through trees to join a track way. Turn right, and shortly cross a stile by a gate into Lamberhurst and the A21. Bear left across the busy road onto a waymarked tarmac path behind a house to a stile. Proceed uphill on a defined grassy path to a further stile, then pass through a vineyard to join a concrete drive and keep ahead to the B-road. Turn left and keep left at the road junction back to the pub.

National Trust parkland at Scotney Castle

**Walk No. 21**

# The Bull Inn, Linton

Standing halfway up Linton Hill beside the A229, this fine part-timbered hostelry was once an old coaching inn where horses were changed and rested after the long, steep climb. The date etched on the façade records 1674 but is believed to be much older, as the existence of a priest hole in the building seems to indicate. Like the magnificent white mansion in Linton Park, the Bull enjoys unrivalled views across the expanse of the Weald from its lawned rear garden, a delight on summer days. Being on a hill, the bar areas are on different levels, the higher restaurant area once served as the village post office until it closed in 1982 and was incorporated in to the inn. The wood panelled bar serves three carpeted and comfortably furnished rooms, all of which have par-panelled walls, beams and some exposed standing timbers. The lower, more characterful bar boasts a splendid inglenook with welcoming winter log fire, which reflects off the horse brasses and shiny brass plates adorning the overmantel beam.

Shepherd Neame acquired this inn, a former Whitbread house, which is good news for lovers of Kentish ales. Regularly featured are Master Brew, Kent's Best and Late Red.

A carefully considered food policy means the emphasis during the week is good pub food serving "the best carvery in Kent" all day Sundays. The carvery appears again as a special treat on Thursday evenings for all those confined to the church or allotments on Sundays. There are nine "lite-bite" appetisers to choose from, Kentish ploughman's, homemade pies and puddings, fajitas, rib eyes and rumps, sandwiches, baked potatoes and fresh ciabattas. Weekday food service is from 12 noon till 2.30 pm and 6 till 9 pm, 12 noon till 9 pm at weekends.

This is a pub that welcomes walkers with friendly staff and ever open doors.

Hours are 11 am till 11 pm, Monday to Saturday and 12 noon till 10.30 pm Sundays

Children are welcome and dogs in the bar area.

Telephone: 01622 743612.

## Walk No. 21

Village and pub are located on the A229 Maidstone to Hastings road, 3½ miles south of Maidstone. Postcode: ME17 4AW.

Approx. distance of walks: 4 miles. OS Map No. 148/136 TQ 755/502.

The inn has a small rear car park and the village has a free car park adjacent to the church.

*An enjoyable ramble across the greensand ridge through unspoilt parkland and orchards, affording good views across the Weald. The peaceful churchyard of the idyllically located St Andrew's Church at Boughton Monchelsea is a delight, overlooking a fine deer park and the expanse of the Weald. Easy going underfoot it is an ideal walk for all the family. Boughton Monchelsea Place is privately owned and only open to the public by arrangement for certain functions. The grounds can be visited on some dates in the summer. Tel 01622 743 120.*

1. From the pub, turn right along the footway and soon carefully cross the busy A229 to follow the Greensand Way through the churchyard. Pass through a metal swing gate onto a grassy fenced path, cross the driveway to the magnificent Linton Park House – known as the Citadel of Kent with the Weald as its garden – and pass through a further gate to follow a defined path along the edge of woodland. Eventually drop down some steps and across a lane onto the driveway to Loddington Oast, waymarked Boughton Church. Keep left following the worn and well marked path through orchards via a stile to a gate onto a lane.

2. To visit Boughton Church, pass through the gate and turn right, otherwise follow the narrow path left and shortly cross the lane onto a waymarked woodland path beside a high stone wall. Exit the trees, follow yellow arrow slightly right across a field, pass through a gateway and across the driveway to Boughton Monchelsea Place. Follow markers onto a grassy path between fields to a stile. Maintain direction on the worn path (good Wealdon views) to a scrub area and crossing of paths. Turn right down the field edge, ignore stile on your left and continue steeply downhill passing farm buildings on the left. Soon the path bears left into the next field then turn right along field edge to cross a stile, a plank bridge and a further stile into parkland on your right.

3. Bear half-left through pasture, pass to the left of a small lake, disregard stile on your left and proceed half-right to a stile and a lane. Turn right, pass Keepers Cottage and turn left at a T-junction opposite a white house. Shortly climb a stile beside double wooden gates on your right and walk along the right-hand edge of a field to a plank bridge and stile into coppiced woodland. Follow a well waymarked path, keeping left at a T-junction of paths and shortly emerge from the wood. Head downhill to a stile and continue ahead on a wide track through an orchard to a stile by a gate onto a lane.

4. Turn left, then at the end of a wire fenced area, turn right onto an arrowed path through scrub to a stile. Keep straight on through Linton Park, following the line of an old fence to a stile near a lake. Proceed ahead through the park to a stile and cross the A229 onto the footway. Turn right and follow the road uphill back to the pub.

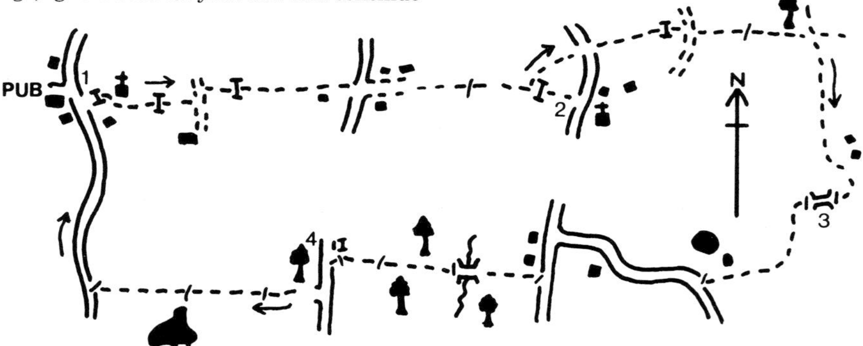

# The Gate Inn, Marshside

Set beside a lane surrounded by farmland and marshes, this splendid, unspoilt retreat is well worth seeking out. Rather than a farm gate, the pub name reputedly refers to the old gateway to the Archbishop of Canterbury's manor house at the nearby hamlet of Ford. The junction outside the pub is known as Boyden Gate. The reasons for a visit here lie behind its flower-adorned, yet unassuming façade and within the extraordinary garden. An unpretentious atmosphere fills the two charmingly rustic connecting rooms which have quarry-tiled floors, a central brick fireplace with open fire, a delightful mix of old, sturdy scrubbed pine tables, chairs and stripped cushioned pews. Hops hang from the ceiling beams and a variety of photographs and prints of village people and scenes in bygone days line the rough plastered walls. The traditional pub charm is enhanced with the absence of piped music, just the lively chatter of 'locals' and a selection of time-honoured pub games. There is a pond, and a river in the garden and picnic benches amongst the apple trees.

The pub is owned by Shepherd Neame and dispenses well conditioned Master Brew, Spitfire and seasonal variations from the brewer.

Homely bar food, served throughout opening hours using fresh local produce, is listed on a regularly changing blackboard menu and may feature tomato soup, bacon and mushroom torpedo, steak, salad and jacket potato, ploughman's and unusual sandwiches including the famous black pudding filling served with lots of pickles, spicy sausage hotpot, burgers, bean and vegetable hotpot and ratatouille flan. Free range eggs and local vegetables are sold over the bar.

Opening times are from 11 am till 2.30 pm (Saturday 3 pm) and 6 till 11 pm. Sunday 12 noon till 4.30 pm and 7 till 10.30 pm.

There is a family room and children are also allowed in the eating area of the bar. Dogs allowed too.

Telephone: 01227 860498.

## Walk No. 22

Hamlet lies 2 miles north of the A28 at Upstreet, between Canterbury and Margate. Postcode: CT34 EB.

Approx. distance of walk: 4 miles. OS Map. No. 150 TR 220/657.

Parking is limited at the inn, spaces can be found along the lane.

*A pleasant marshland walk, yet despite being quite flat the views over the surrounding countryside are extensive, taking in nearby villages and hamlets. Sarre windmill can be seen for much of the walk and with a steady wind the sails can be seen moving open daily). Also of interest locally are the ruins of St Mary's church at Reculver*

1. Turn right out of the inn, then in a short distance climb the waymarked stile on your left and proceed to a further stile by a dyke. Keep ahead to follow the stream and cross two more stiles before reaching a footbridge on your left. Do not cross the bridge, instead turn right across the field to cross another footbridge, then turn right and proceed to a stile and lane. Bear left and follow the narrow lane with a dyke to your left for some distance, before turning left along a waymarked bridleway (Gilling Drove). Follow this track which eventually becomes a footpath through some trees to a footbridge over a river.

2. Turn left following the Wantsum Walk, ignore two wooden bridges to your left and eventually turn left through a waymarked iron gate onto a track way. Continue along this track following the markers and pass through an iron gate onto a road. Take the lane opposite signposted, Herne, then after a short distance take the footpath left just beyond Peggotty Cottage. Pass over a wooden footbridge and keep ahead, passing behind buildings on your left. Follow markers to cross two stiles to the right of a thatched cottage and a further stile down to a road. Turn right, then at a T-junction turn left back to the Gate Inn.

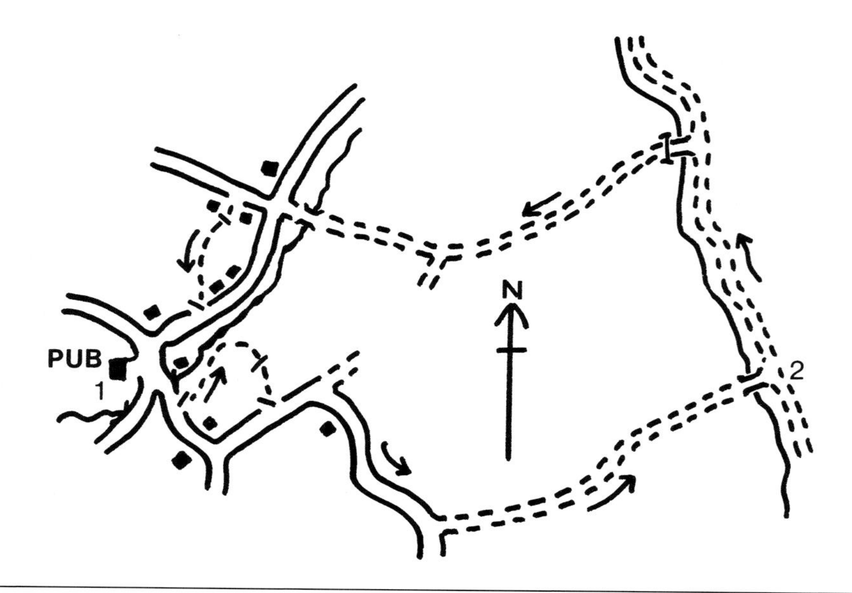


The sketch maps in this book are not necessarily to scale but have been drawn to show maximum amount of detail.

# The George Inn, Newnham

Newnham means 'new settlement', but the village in fact is very old with a Norman motte and bailey castle and some fine old buildings, including the splendid 16th-century George Inn opposite the church. Originally built in 1540 as a farm dwelling it was later split into three cottages, becoming an inn in 1718 and acquired by the local Shepherd Brewery in 1887. The distinctive, mellow brick and tile-hung façade hides a most delightful and lovingly cared for interior. A long wood-panelled bar runs the length of the series of character rooms which are furnished and decorated to a very high standard. Polished wooden floors are strewn with fine rugs and laid out with an interesting mix of dining tables and chairs, upholstered mahogany settles, long oak refectory tables, farmhouse chairs and stripped wooden benches. Hops adorn the ceiling and bar, while various tasteful prints, paintings, polished copper, farm memorabilia, and unusual collections of butterflies, clay pipes and glass ware decorate the walls. Added touches include an abundance of fresh and dried flower arrangements, evening candle-light and good log burning fires, one in an enormous inglenook, which warm this most relaxing place. The sheltered garden overlooking sheep pastures is used annually for the village fete.

Still owned by Shepherd Neame the pub serves a selection of their ales including Master Brew, Spitfire and Late Red.

Discerning diners come from far afield to sample the varied and imaginative home-cooked food. Served Monday to Saturday 12 noon till 2.30 pm and 7 till 9.30 pm, Sunday 12 noon till 6 pm and 7 till 9.30 pm. Regular menu choices include moules, chicken liver pate, steak and kidney pie, pasta of the day, smoked chicken and basil tartlets, chilli, fillet steak with port and cream, sandwiches and a good variety of ploughman's. Excellent and more elaborate daily specials include warm salad of duck breast with walnut oil dressing or half shoulder of lamb with honey glaze, pan fried calves liver with bacon and onion and pot roasted pheasant with wine and chestnuts.

Opening times are from 11 am till 3 pm and 6.30 till 11 pm, Sunday 12 noon till 10.30 pm.

Well behaved children are welcome inside and have their own menu. Dogs in garden only.

Telephone: 01795 890237.

## Walk No. 23

Village is located on a minor road near Doddington, 3 miles south-west of the A2 near Faversham. Postcode: ME9 0LL.

Approx. distance of walk: 5½ miles. OS Map No. 149 TQ 955/576.

The inn has its own car park.

*A varied and easy going walk incorporating woodland, parkland and open farmland on good farm tracks and field paths. Three interesting churches can be visited on route. The 10 acres of tranquil gardens at Doddington Place are open on certain days throughout the summer.*

1. Leave the inn, turn left along the footway and take the waymarked path left beside Quince Cottage to a stile. Bear diagonally left uphill across pasture to a stile in the field corner and turn right along a metalled driveway. Pass a sawmill, keep left at a fork, pass in front of the gates to Sharsted Court and follow the track to a stile beside a gate into Sharsted Wood. Proceed ahead along a splendid woodland drive, then after about 200 yards turn right onto a wide pathway which soon curves left through the trees, eventually reaching a stile and lane beside a cottage.
2. Turn right, then at the T-junction, turn left and take the waymarked path right beside a bungalow. Follow the field edge to the end of a fence, then bear slightly left across a field passing waymarker post at the end of a hedge and continue on a worn path to a stile. Keep left-handed, pass through an old arrowed gateway and shortly join a track. Proceed ahead, bear left with fingerpost in front of a converted oast house and follow the metalled driveway to a quiet lane.
3. Turn right along the lane to a waymarked path left. Cross a field to a tree-lined hedgerow, following it behind Great Higham Farm, then continue along a line of telegraph poles and a field edge to join a worn path which soon curves right towards trees. At a crossroads of arrowed paths, turn left, cross a stile by a gate and keep left through pasture to a stile in the field corner. Turn right along the field edge, cross a stile (ignore stile right) and maintain direction through the perimeter of an orchard, bearing right beside houses onto a track to a lane.
4. Turn left, then shortly turn right onto a waymarked grassy track between two bungalows. As the track bears left, proceed straight across the field to a stile, then cross pasture to a further stile and continue ahead to a lane opposite Doddington Church. Cross over onto the driveway between the church and the Old Vicarage and keep ahead along a grassy track to a metal kissing gate and a fork of paths. Head straight across parkland towards Doddington Place, pass through a further kissing gate and continue in front of the house, soon to keep right of the driveway, downhill to a kissing gate beside the main gates. Turn left along the footway for a ¼ mile back into Newnham.

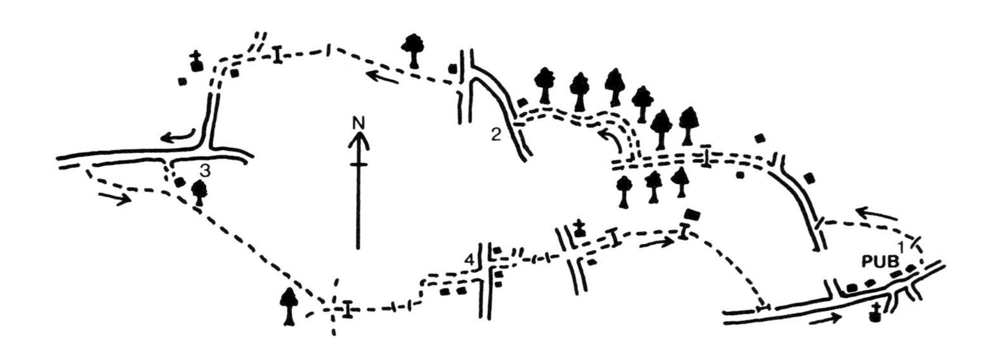

**Walk No. 24**

# The Crown, Otford

This attractive white-painted pub from the Elizabethan era dates back to 1560 and has been converted several times over the years before returning to an ale house in 1860. It is picturesquely set at the top of the High Street opposite the village pond – the only area of water in England designated as a listed building – the remains of an old Archbishops of Canterbury palace and the fine restored Norman church of St Bartholomew. Inside a cosy warm atmosphere prevails in the bars, which have a wealth of exposed beams, upright and wall timbers and two huge inglenook fireplaces. Old foreign bank notes adorn the beams of the dining area along with a selection of old hotel keys and a replica knight in armour. A door from the public bar leads out to the enclosed rear garden. The neat dining area has seating for 32.

In 2010 this busy establishment was owned by Punch Taverns. Ales usually available are Harveys Best, Woodfords Wherry and their own Otford Crown brewed by Westerham.

Food service, Monday and Tuesday 12 noon to 3 pm only. Wednesday to Saturday 12 noon till 3 pm and 6 pm till 9 pm and Sunday 12 noon till 5 pm. A comprehensive set of menus list the home-cooked food. Lunch time fare includes a choice of sandwiches, filled jackets, steak and kidney pudding, game pie, ham, egg and chips, cod and chips, salads, pasta, sausage and mash and pan fried salmon. They also have a take-away service for food and ale. Desserts change daily but could include homemade favourites like apple crumble and real ice cream. Sundays are particularly busy as they serve a wide selection of home-cooked roast meats, all provided by the local butcher and vegetables come from the local green grocer. They make their own Yorkshire pudding and serve pork, beef, chicken, turkey or lamb in small, medium or large portions all accompanied by roast potatoes, new potatoes and a medley of vegetables. Booking is recommended. Senior citizen specials run Monday to Thursday lunchtimes. Friday is fish day.

Opening times 12 noon till 11 pm, weekends all day 11 am till 11 pm.

Children are welcome in the dining area, where they have their own menu. Dogs are allowed in the bar and only in the dining area by prior arrangement.

Telephone: 01959 522847.

## Walk No. 24

Village is located in the Darent Valley on the A225 Sevenoaks to Dartford road and convenient to junction 5 on the M25. Postcode: TN14 5PQ.

Approx. distance of walk: 6 miles. OS Map No. 147 TQ 528/593.

It is best to park in the free car park beside the village hall along the High Street.

*Although quite long and challenging, this most enjoyable rural ramble explores the Darent Valley and the well marked farmland and woodland paths that crisscross an unspoilt area of the North Downs. Note, there are a few strength-sapping steep climbs, rewarding by splendid country views and the going is generally good underfoot. Lullingstone Castle and Roman Villa are close by at Eynsford.*

1. From the village car park turn right – Crown lies to the left by the pond – along the High Street and soon take the arrowed Darent Valley Path, along side the river on a tarmac drive. Follow yellow arrow beside Little Oast to stile, then keep left-handed through pasture parallel with river to a further stile. Maintain direction, cross farm track via two stiles, and then proceed along right-hand edge of field to a stile in the corner. Continue on a narrow fenced path through a golf course to a walk-through stile and metalled track. Turn right, then at an arrowed post turn left, waymarked Shoreham and cross a cricket field before resuming route through a golf course to a lane.

2. Turn right uphill, pass beneath the railway, then at the main road take the waymarked bridleway to the right of Copt Hall opposite. Shortly, keep left at a fork of paths to follow an established path through woodland and steeply ascend scarp slope of the North Downs via wooden steps. Keep ahead at a crossing of paths, soon enter an open field and bear half-left on worn paths towards barns. Join a track, bear right then left through the farm and follow fenced bridleway to a waymarked stile on your left. Climb the stile, head half-right through a gateway and soon reach a stile preceeding woodland. Descend steeply to a stile and cross a golf course on a grassy path to a further stile.

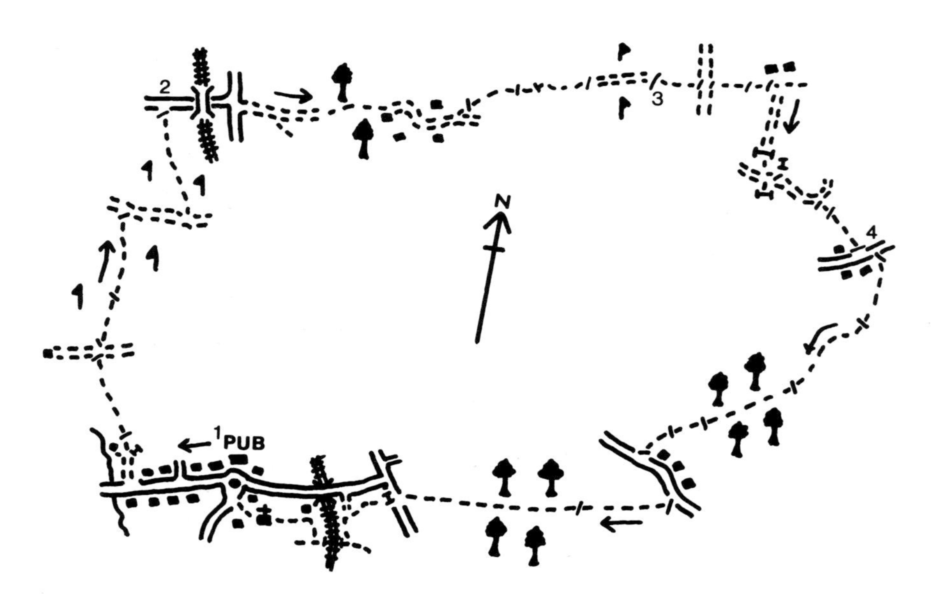

3. Climb steeply through pasture, cross a farm track via two stiles and proceed on a good path uphill to a stile close to a large house and the hamlet of Romney Street. Keep left-handed along fencing, cross another stile, then turn right along wide bridleway and pass beside a small metal gate. Take the path waymarked Eastdown, across a stile between two gates, follow muddy track way to where it veers sharp left then keep ahead (yellow arrow) to a stile. Proceed right-handed through pasture, climb a stile onto a narrow path and descend to a stile and lane.

4. Turn left, then in a few yards climb the stile on the right beside a gate and keep right beside fencing, soon to cross the centre of pasture on a path to a stile. Steeply descend through scrub and trees to a stile and follow path through woodland. Continue over three more stiles to a lane, then turn left passing Paines Farm and shortly climb the arrowed stile to your right. Keep right - trig point to the left - cross a stile into woodland and begin to descend along the North Downs Way towards Otford. On reaching a road cross over, bear right along the footway, then pass through a wooden swing gate on your left to follow yellow arrows through 'Chalk Pit'. At a metalled path turn right, then shortly left along the right-hand side of a brick scout hut. Follow worn path through trees to a further tarmac path, turn right and carefully cross the railway line crossing via two stiles. Turn immediately right, then bear left beside the station car park and proceed to and through churchyard back to the A225, the village pond and The Crown.

The River Darent near Otford

Walk No. 25

# Rose & Crown, Perry Wood

Historic Perry Wood hides a wealth of footpaths, the site of old Shottenden Mill, an Iron Age earthworks, the famous Pulpit – magnificent views across the Kentish countryside – and the friendly Rose & Crown. Dating from the 16th-century, this attractive building is quietly located beside a narrow lane and is a particular favourite with families in summer for its secluded rear garden, complete with play area, barbecue and bat and ball trap pitch. Inside, the welcoming beamed bar is, thankfully, music and game free and boasts two huge brick fireplaces with large timber over mantels and open log fires, an assortment of pub furniture, tapestry covered stools and pew seating. Down a few steps is the snug bar which is reputedly haunted by Hammond John Smith, who was murdered at the pub in 1889, dying from twelve stab wounds he suffered following an argument about cutting and tying corn. Beyond the snug is the restaurant area which features exposed wall timbers, a grandfather clock and collections of bygones and old photographs.

The pub is a freehouse serving at least four real ales at any one time usually Harveys Best, Adnams South Wold plus two guests.

Popular home-cooked bar food is served daily from 12 noon till 2 pm and 6.30 till 9 pm, except Sunday evening. In summer food is served on Saturdays from 12 noon till 9 pm, and Sunday 12 noon till 6 pm. The menu lists a choice of jacket potatoes, mixed grill, steak and ale pie, omelettes, ploughman's and a range of sandwiches. Daily specials may include leek and potato soup, Kent fish pie, liver and bacon, sausage, bacon and mushroom casserole or grilled whole plaice. A few additions are featured on the evening menu e.g. local game in season, lamb medallions and salmon steak. Pudding choices range from apple crumble and sticky toffee pudding to bread and butter pudding.

Opening times are from 11.30 am (12 noon Sunday) till 3 pm and 6.30 till 11 pm. The pub is closed Monday evenings. Summer time open all day at weekends.

Telephone: 01227 752214.

Perry Wood Nature Reserve can be reached by following signs to Old Wives Lees and then Selling from the A28 near Shalmsford Street, 4 miles south-west of Canterbury. Pub is signed from Selling. Postcode: ME13 9RY.

Approx. distance of walk: 2 miles. OS Map No. 149 TR 041/552.

The inn has plenty of parking spaces.

*An enjoyable family woodland stroll, affording good cameo views across splendid countryside. Easy going, but can be muddy in places. The nature reserve covers 150 acres and is one of the most unspoilt areas of woodland in Kent, providing a good opportunity to see a variety of woodland birds.*

1. From the pub turn right onto a bridleway and soon pass close to an information board full of interesting facts about Perry Wood and its wildlife. Follow the established path around a cottage, then at a junction of paths proceed ahead with blue arrow. Keep to main path around the base and fringe of the common land with good views. Curve left with a path around the hillside, go across the crossroads of paths, then keep left at a further junction following blue arrows.
2. On reaching a post with three blue arrows, bear right onto a narrow path through coppice, downhill to a crossing of tracks near a cottage. Continue ahead, re-enter woodland and follow arrows to a lane. Turn left and take the second waymarked path right, into the visitors car park. Cross the centre of the car park, and join the arrowed path passing between a pond and house to cross a driveway onto a lane.
3. Turn left at the fingerpost, cross the lane onto a driveway and pass through a gate. Beyond another gate keep left at a bungalow and follow the narrow path behind a large garden to a stile. Enter an old orchard with a bungalow to your left, bear diagonally left passing to the right of the property and between two sheds to a stile by a telegraph pole and cross a lane onto a bridleway. Keep right through woodland (blue arrows), then right at a fork and shortly reach a crossroads of path. Turn left and follow the path (can be muddy) to the lane opposite the pub.

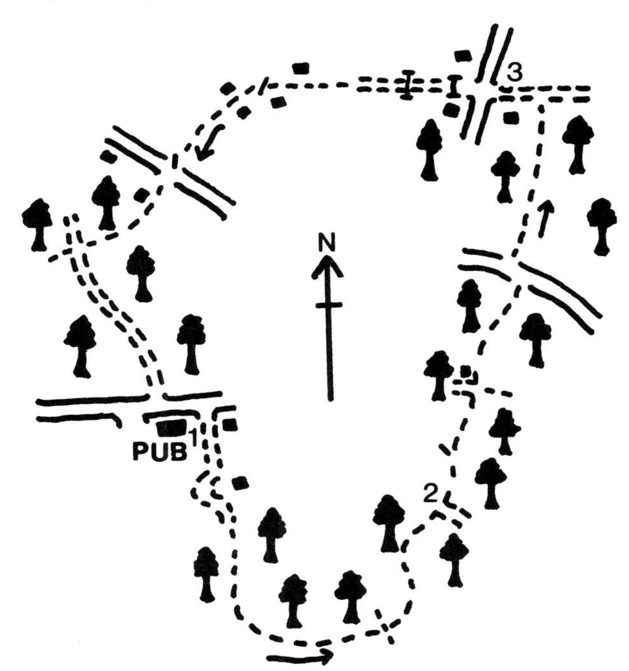

**Walk No. 26**

# The Duck, Pett Bottom

Originally a shepherd's cottage built in 1621, this very attractive long, low tile-hung building enjoys a splendid isolated position along a narrow lane with unspoilt rural valley views. It has been a pub for over 170 years and among its more recent customers was author Ian Fleming, who wrote the James Bond books and who lived locally. The Duck was featured in his book 'Moonraker'. The present name is derived from the directive above its low doorway, which advises people to 'duck'. This classic country pub remains delightfully traditional in both layout and atmosphere its lounge bar and adjacent restaurant being thankfully game free. The bar is warmed by an open log fire in a fine 17th-century fireplace and is neatly furnished with stripped tables, wheel-back chairs and the odd pew. Fresh flowers and candles top the tables here and in the restaurant area, enhancing the mellow, intimate dining ambience that prevails in the evening. There is a secluded picnic-bench filled garden to the side.

This freehouse offers the choice of Greene King IPA, Shepherd Neame Master Brew and Young's Bitter, augmented at times by regular beer festivals.

Food service Monday to Saturday is 12 noon till 2.30 pm and 6.30 till 9.30 pm, Sunday 12 noon till 4 pm and 6.30 till 9 pm. The main menu features starters like venison and free range chicken parfait with toast and chutney and crispy breaded brie wedges with a redcurrant and white wine sauce. Mains listed are roast Oxford sandy and black pork served with crackling and quince jelly, pan roasted pheasant beast with black pudding and white currant sauce, 'The Duck Inn' mixed grill, homemade 100% beef burgers, beer battered cod, slow roasted barbecue ribs and spinach and ricotta cannelloni. Sunday lunch offers a selection of traditional roasts along with homemade pies and fresh fish dishes. Booking is essential at busy times to avoid disappointment.

Opening hours are weekdays 12 noon till 3 pm and 6 till 11 pm, Saturday 12 noon till 11 pm and Sunday 12 noon till 10 pm.

Children and dogs are welcome both in the pub and the garden.

Telephone: 01227 830354.

Hamlet is sign-posted from the village of Bridge, 3 miles south-east of Canterbury. Postcode: CT4 5PB.

Approx. distance of the walk: 5 miles. OS Map No. 150 TR 161/520.

The pub has a car park to the side.

*A delightful gentle walk through apple orchards and along well waymarked farmland paths and tracks. Easy going with fine rural views. Nearby is Howletts Zoo set in 55 acres of parkland and home to the world's largest family of gorillas, amongst many other rare animals (open daily).*

1. Take the waymarked path left where the car park joins the lane and gently climb into woodland. At a T-junction of paths turn left follow the defined path to a stile at the woodland edge. Proceed ahead along the lane of power cables, shortly to bear half-left downhill across an open field to a fingerpost and lane. Turn right, pass Little Eaton farm and take the next arrowed path right beside a tall hedge. Bear off left with yellow marker through the hedge into an orchard and keep left-handed beside another tall hedge. At a track turn right and shortly climb the stile on your left beyond a wide trackway. Continue ahead, cross a track and walk between lines of apple trees towards a wooded chalk bank.
2. Keep left of the wood along the orchard edge, then shortly turn left onto a track beside a plantation of apple trees, follow the track right, ignore stile to your left remaining on the track around the orchard edge. Turn right just beyond a line of tall tree between orchards and follow the earth track left then right out of the orchard. Pass farm sheds and follow grass-centred track through open farmland, bearing left down to Lenhall Farm.
3. Pass between barns and bear right onto a metalled drive, following it to a lane. Keep left, then just before reaching a bridge and Bishopbourne sign, bear off right onto a wide track way, (not waymarked). Shortly turn right along a hedged grass-centred trackway. Where the tracks bear sharply left, continue ahead on a defined path to a fence stile and pass through a narrow stretch of woodland. Proceed ahead, shortly to follow the right-hand edge of two crop fields to a lane.
4. Turn right, soon bear left onto a signed grass-centred track and gently climb along the edge of woodland to a further lane. Turn left following the lane steeply downhill. Pass a crossroads of driveways, then pass through a waymarked gate on your right into pasture. Keep right-handed to a stile, cross a driveway onto a track and soon climb a stile beyond the entrance to Gorsley House. Follow the narrow hedged path to a further stile, pass in front of a large garage and continue ahead on a defined path along the woodland fringe. Enter the wood, then at a small post with yellow arrows, turn left retracing your steps back to the pub.

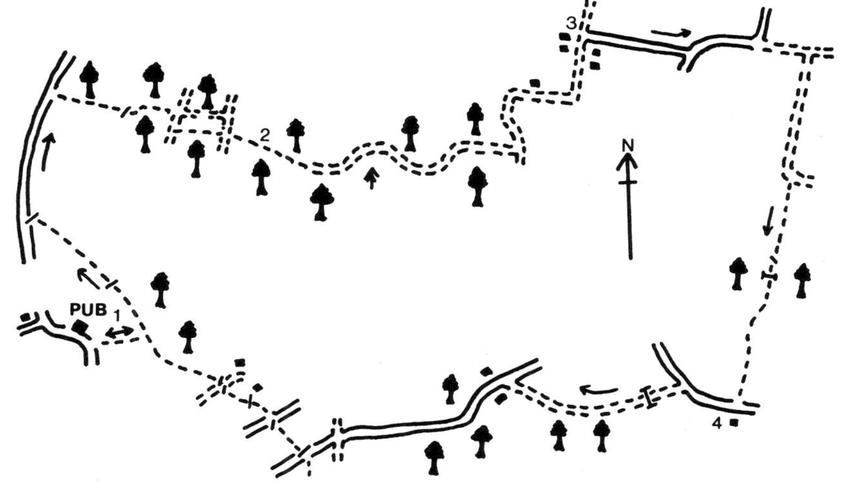

Walk No. 27

# The Black Horse, Pluckley

Pluckley is reputedly the most haunted village in the country, claiming at least twelve ghosts. One such spirit resides at The Black Horse in the form of a poltergeist and is thought to be that of Jessie Brooks, killed by a ball in the skittle alley when the pub was located elsewhere in the village. The building dominates the neat village street and dates from 1470 when it was a moated farmhouse. It became a pub over 160 years ago and is noted for the 19th-century. 'Dering' arched windows which characterise the village. A few years ago the pub featured in the TV series Darling Buds of May, which was filmed around the village. The cosy and atmospheric interior comprises a series of inter-connected rooms featuring exposed brickwork and part pine-panelled walls – some draped with old tapestries – ochre coloured beamed ceiling, some upright timbers, a vast inglenook, an impressive carved stone fireplace and an assortment of comfortable furnishings. Fine weather seating can be found in the large orchard garden with picnic benches and village views.

This friendly establishment owned by Enterprise Inns, dispenses Adnams Bitter, Fullers London Pride and Shepherd Neame Master Brew on hand pump.

A wide-ranging menu is served daily from 12 noon till 2.30 pm and 6 till 9 pm, Sunday 12 noon till 5 pm. Generously served dishes include country soup, salads, filled jacket potatoes, ham and eggs, steak and kidney pie, mixed grill, steaks, local trout, chilli, moussaka, fish and chips, seafood pie, chicken curry, lemon sole and a good range of 'doorstep' sandwiches and ploughman's. Vegetarian choices include vegetable burgers and mushroom and nut fettucini. Sunday roasts.

Weekday opening times are from 11.30 am till 11 pm, Sunday 12 noon till 10.30 pm.

Children are welcome in the dining area and have their own menu. Dogs are allowed in the bar on a lead.

Telephone: 01233 842948.

## Walk No. 27

Village is located on the Charing to Smarden road, 3 miles south-west of Charing off the A20. Postcode: TN27 0QS.

Approx. distance of walk: 4½ miles. OS Map No. 137 TQ 926/455.

Parking is available at the front of the inn.

*This delightful rural stroll explores the beautiful countryside featured in the book and TV series the 'Darling Buds of May'. Orchard, field and farmland paths are well waymarked, easy going and offer fine views of both the North Downs and across the expanse of the Weald.*

1. From the pub turn right, then right again at the T-junction and follow the road uphill for a short distance to pick up the waymarked Greensand Way, arrowed right across a playing field. Pass through a gap in the hedge (waymarker post), and go across a farm track onto a footpath through an orchard. Proceed ahead at a crossroad of tracks along the left-hand edge of a further orchard, passing in front of Sheerland Farm. Cross farm drive, follow markers and shortly cross a lane onto a narrow path between a wall and a garden. Climb a stile, keep left-handed through pasture, cross a path via two stiles and maintain course to a swing gate in field corner. Follow defined waymarked path through an orchard, cross a track and stile, then turn left around the orchard edge to a stile in the hedgerow. Bear diagonally left across an open field, keeping left of the church to cross a track and shortly drop down some steps onto a lane in Little Chart.

2. Turn left, cross the lane and join a track between Rockhurst Bungalow and Little Chart Mill. Pass through a gate, keep to the right-hand edge of a field, ignore footbridge on the right and soon bear right with green arrow onto a track to a stile beside a gate. Cross a further stile and proceed into Chart Court Farm, keeping right at a fork of tracks (yellow arrows) towards a ruined church. Soon bear off right, pass through gap in the hedge into the old churchyard and keep left to a road.

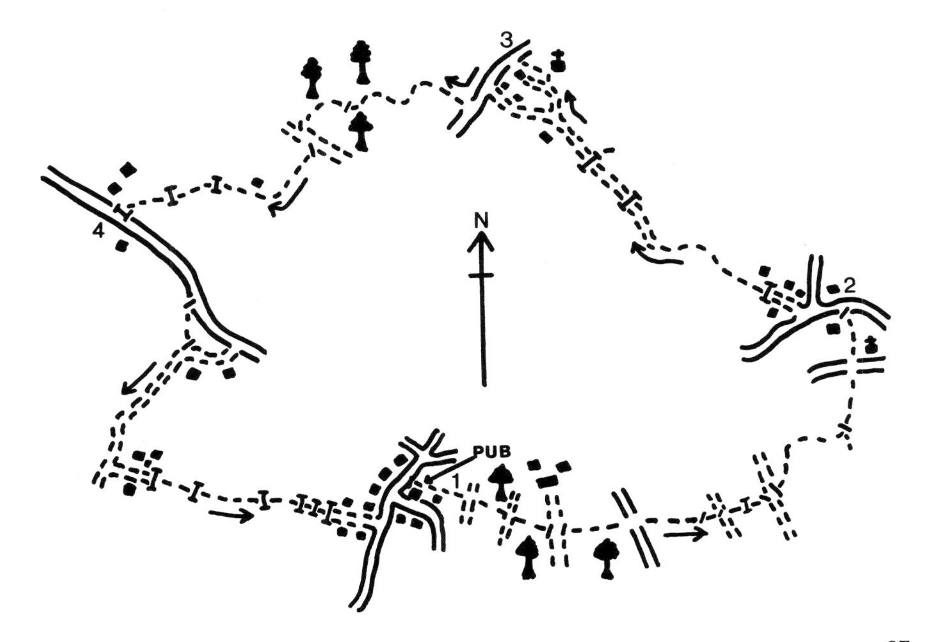

3. Turn left along the verge and shortly cross the road onto a waymarked path along the right-hand edge of an orchard. Bear left in a further orchard, then turn right onto wide track through the trees and bear left to a stile into woodland. Follow path through trees to a track, turn left, then in a few yards cross a stile on your right and head straight across an open field. Turn right with waymarker along field edge, join a gassy track and pass a derelict building to a gate. Continue to a further gate and a lane.

4. Turn left, pass Pivington Farm in 200 yards lookout for a stile in the hedgerow on your right. Bear left up a grassy bank towards cottages, cross a stile and turn right onto a track in front of the cottages and remain on this old established route downhill to Elvey Farm. Turn left along the driveway through the farmyard to a gate and rejoin the Greensand Way. Keep right-handed through pasture, pass through a gate and keep to the defined waymarked path uphill across fields via four gates to join a track leading to a road. Turn left, then right back into Pluckley to the pub.

Typical Kentish oast house near Pluckley

Converted oast house at Levey Farm on the Greensand Way

Ruins of St. Mary's Church beside Chart Court Farm

Walk No. 28

# The Ringlestone Inn, Ringlestone

Isolated high up on top of the North Downs beside a now metalled stretch of the ancient Pilgrims Way lies this unspoilt gem of a country pub. Built in 1533, the Ringlestone was originally owned by the church and used as a hospice for travelling monks, who for many years farmed the land around it. It became one of the early 'ale houses' around 1615 and the original part of the inn remains much as it did then and the inscription carved in 1632 on the impressive English oak sideboard proclaiming 'A Ryghte Joyouse and welcome greetynge to ye all' is still very true to this day. Three atmospheric inter-connecting rooms radiate around the bar, all featuring brick and flint walls and floors, a wealth of oak beams, a huge inglenook fireplace with blazing winter wood burner and a delightful assortment of rustic furniture. On dark winter evenings the charming ambience is enhanced by candlelight. A later addition to the pub is the rear dining room and food servery. Attractive and peaceful summer garden with raised lawn and a rockery with waterfalls and fountain.

This former freehouse has been acquired by Shepherd Neame and in 2010 they were serving Master Brew and Late Red or Spitfire. They also offer a large selection of English fruit wines.

Excellent food is served seven days a week. Lunch time Monday to Saturday 12 noon till 2 pm Sunday 12 noon till 3 pm Eveninghs Monday to Thursday 7 pm till 9 pm Friday to Sunday 6 pm till 9 pm. The menu includes slow-roasted pork belly, lamb shank marinated in red wine, 'Ringlestone pies', baby back ribs, fish in elderflower wine plus other fresh fish dishes like red snapper or sea bass. The puddings to delight 'Billy Bunter' include spotted dick, sticky toffee pudding, apple crumble and jam roly-poly topped with a choice of twenty ice cream flavours.

Children are welcome and they have a play area set aside with, as a further attraction, a barn owl and a hawk . Dogs on leads are also welcome.

Telephone: 01622 859900.

Hamlet is located 1½ miles east of the B2163 Hollingbourne to Sittingbourne road. Turn right at water tower 1 mile north of Hollingbourne. Postcode: ME17 1NX.

Approx. distance of walk: 5½ miles. OS Map No. 148 TQ 879/ 557.

There is a large car park at the inn.

*A fine walk on the North Downs, across open farmland and along the North Downs/Pilgrims Way, a scenic and established long-distance path that links Farnham in Surrey to Dover. One fairly steep climb but generally easy going underfoot. Good rural views from the North Downs escarpment. Leeds Castle, described as the "loveliest castle in the world" is only a few miles away. Built on two islands in the middle of a lake it has been beautifully restored and furnished and is set in 500 acres of landscaped park.*

1. Climb the stile on the right beside the inn and follow the waymarked path along the right-hand hedge to the rear of the inn. Shortly bear left across the field to a stile in the far left-hand corner and a quiet lane. Cross over to an arrowed path across farm land, keeping the hedge on your right into a field by a copse. Turn left at the end of the copse to the edge of a paddock and a stile on the left. Bear right across the field to a stile in the corner and turn right onto a track into a farmyard.

2. Pass through two metal gates, climb the stile ahead and follow the path between a fence and hedge downhill. Cross two stiles on your left, then bear right down the field edge and remain on the defined path down to an established track – The Pilgrims Way/NorthDowns Way. Turn right and remain on the track to where it becomes metalled. Turn right onto a gravel track, climb gently uphill and soon bear off right with yellow markers, uphill through a small copse and along the left-hand edge of a field to a stile.

3. Keep to the left-hand path uphill through the edge of a beech wood to a stile, then cross a large open field on a defined path, heading between a cottage and a concrete reservoir to a lane. Cross over into a field and bear diagonally right on a path and pass down the left-hand side of a copse to two stiles. Bear half-right across another field to a lane near a house.

4. Turn left then shortly right along a lane signposted 'camping – tents only', pass the entrance to a house on the right and proceed uphill to cross a stile on your right. Proceed across a field to a further stile, then bear diagonally left across a field to a stile in the corner next to woodland. Follow the path through a wooden gate onto a track down to the lane, opposite the inn.

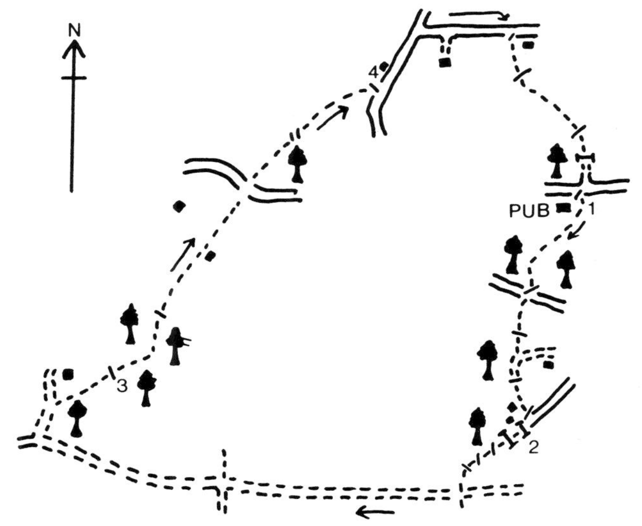

**Walk No. 29**

# The White Cliffs Hotel, St Margarets at Cliffe

The White Cliffs Hotel, formerly the Cliffe Tavern, is a series of attractive 17th-century Kentish clapboard-and-brick buildings, located opposite the Norman church in the centre of the village. The tall, three-storey main building houses the bars and a few of the bedrooms. The front bar has white painted walls with black painted timber and is simply furnished with dark wood 'pub' tables and dark green velour padded wall benches and stools heated by a roaring winter fire. There are a few local prints on the wall one a noticeable World War II picture of an aerial dogfight In general the bar has a pleasant, friendly atmosphere. The décor changes in the smartly refurbished separate restaurant area called The Bay. Behind the hotel is a pleasant re-designed garden area with tables and chairs.

Regular ales on offer are Fullers London Pride and Adnams Bitter.

In something of a food policy statement the management declare that they source ingredients that are "local, fresh, organic and sustainable" and they must be doing something right because they have been awarded two rosettes in the Good Food Guide. The menu is changed monthly and in between times augmented with daily specials. Typically starters might include Sussex goats cheese fritters with orange and chilli jam pot and hand dived Shetland scallops with a pumpkin veloute and crispy black pig bacon followed by a roasted haunch of Godmersham venison or poached sea bass with clams. The restaurant is open Monday to Saturday for breakfast 7.30 till 9 am, Sunday 8 till 9.30 am. Lunch every day 12 till 2 pm and dinner 7 till 9 pm.

Children are welcome and have their own menu. Dogs in the garden only.

Accommodation is available in 16 en-suite bedrooms and in family cottages on the site.

Telephone: 01304 852400.

Village is located 1½ miles off the A258 between Dover and Deal.
Postcode: CT15 6AT.

Approx. distance of walk: 7 miles. OS Map No. 138 TR 359/448.

The hotel is in the High Street and has a car park and there is a free public car park behind the church opposite.

*Although quite long, this invigorating walk encompasses the White Cliffs Country Trail which affords views across the Channel to France on a clear day and into the busy harbour at Dover. Good waymarked paths on the return route from Dover. The Pines Garden at St Margarets and South Foreland Lighthouse (NT) can be visited and a short diversion can be made to the splendid castle at Dover.*

1. From the hotel turn left into the High Street and proceed on the footway along Sea Street. Climb a hill, turn right with yellow arrow into St Margarets Road, then in 100 yards turn left onto a concrete track, shortly, follow waymarkers down a long flight of steps and turn right along Foreland Road. Turn left into The Crescent, cross a track (South Foreland Valley) and ascend a chalk track, bearing right onto Lighthouse Down (NT) and the Saxon Shore Way.
2. Join the grassy cliff path with open Channel views and remain on the main defined path, which eventually rejoins the pitted chalk track. Proceed past the windmill, then just before a T-junction with a metalled lane, bear off left with waymarker towards the lighthouse. Follow the coast path sign – Langdon Cliff and Dover – to the left of the lighthouse and soon join the splendid cliff path (White Cliffs Country Trail).
3. Disregard the red arrowed path down to the beach and follow yellow waymarkers inland, skirting Langdon Hole (depression) to join a broad track. Keep left (Nature Reserve) and shortly bear off right up a railed step path up the cliff. Just before a wooden swing gate, bear right uphill onto a path beside a wire fence onto Langdon Cliff, beneath the Coastguard Station. Soon enter the large cliff car park. Keep to the lower terrace and leave via the entrance to reach a hairpin bend.
4. Bear off left with the yellow arrow and follow path downhill to a row of cottages, Descend some steps, then bear right onto a grassy path behind the cottages, parallel with the main road. Pass through scrub towards a bridge, climb some steps up an embankment to a road and turn left to cross the bridge. Take the waymarked path right, cross a stile and continue ahead parallel to the A2 through an army training ground (signs ask you to keep to the arrowed path). Follow yellow arrows along the field edge, then bear left to a gate onto a farm track. Keep left uphill through two gates and a farmyard to the A258.
5. Turn right; follow the footway to a roundabout and taking care cross the busy A2. Pass the entrance to an MOD lane, then shortly climb a waymarked stile on your right into a field. Keep left-handed, cross an arrowed stile on the left and proceed along the right-handed edge of a field towards Bere Farm. Cross the farm driveway via stiles onto a track beside outbuildings to a metal gate. Keep left (yellow arrow) and shortly bear right-handed along the field edge to a stile, then bear diagonally right across a large open field to another stile. Follow defined path across a further field, climb a stile and walk along the left-hand edge of a pasture to a stile flanking a gate. Proceed along an old track, go across a stile and turn right onto a verge, then shortly turn right again at a T-junction back into St Margarets and the hotel.

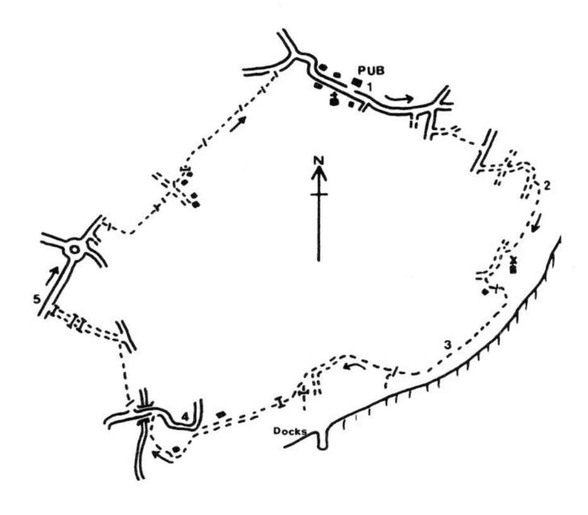

**Walk No. 30**

# The Bell Inn, Smarden

Located beside a country lane just out of the village, this fine old tile-hung building enjoys a pleasant outlook across orchards and sheep pastures. Originally built in 1536 as a farm dwelling it acquired its ale and cider licence in 1630, but bore no name until 1769 when the sign of the 'Bell' was hung. As well as dispensing ale the building housed a blacksmith's forge; a tradition which lasted from a very early period to 1907 and during which time the hostelry offered extensive stabling and hiring facilities. The inn also supplied groceries to the local community after a grocer purchased the inn in 1878; a service that lasted nearly a century. Old-world charm abounds throughout the rambling inter-connecting bars, especially in the older, more intimate Cellar Bar and adjacent cosy room which feature low heavy beams, exposed upright timbers, inglenook fireplaces, brick and flagstone floors, old pews and a mix of candle-topped tables. The main bar is more spacious and rambles through to a lively games area.

Now owned by Shepherd Neam they usually feature Spitfire, Master Brew and Late Red but occasionally others from the SN microbrewery.

Good country fare is served daily 12 noon till 2.30 pm and 6.30 till 9 30 pm (Sunday 8.30 pm). The bar menu list pub staples like beer battered fish and chips, steak and kidney pudding, sausage and mash, lasagne and pie of the day. The à la carte menu features tiger prawns, fish cake with spinach and horseradish, fresh fish and a selection of steak dishes. There is a large beer garden and from June in fine weather a garden bar will operate.

Opening times are 12 noon till 11 pm daily.

This is a child and dog friendly establishment and there is a children's menu.

Telephone: 01233 770283.

**Walk No. 30**

Village is located on a minor road between Pluckley and the A274 near Biddenden. Pub is situated in Bell Lane 1 mile north of the village and is well signposted. Postcode: TN27 88PW.

Approx. distance of walk: 6 miles. OS Map No. 137 TQ 870/430.

The inn has its own car park and there is space along the lane.

*An enjoyable easy and level Wealden walk mostly over farm and pasture land, but can be muddy underfoot after wet weather. Smarden is reputed to be one of the prettiest villages in Kent with a wealth of weather-boarded and old timber-framed cottages, including the former Cloth Hall. The 14th-century church is known as the Barn of Kent because of its width and features a 15th-century tower plus traces of wall paintings. It is well worth lingering awhile in this delightful unspoilt village.*

1. Turn right on leaving the pub and take the first lane right for Smarden, then shortly turn left along a lane signposted Pluckley and Charing. In ¼ mile climb a stile on your right before farm buildings, proceed across a field to a stile, then keep ahead over a playing field and pass through a gap in the hedge to a stile and road. Turn left, then first right and immediately take the arrowed path left to pass beside the village hall. Cross two fields via stiles, go over a footbridge across a stream and follow waymarkers across two more stiles to a lane.

2. Turn right, then immediately left over a stile into a field and bear to the left to go through an iron gate by the farm buildings. Pass to the left of a pond, climb a stile in the far top corner and follow path through woodland to a stile and open field. Cross the stile in the right-hand corner, then bear diagonally left, following the direction of the marker to cross another stile. Turn left and follow round the edge of the field to turn right behind a barn (Wissenden Farm). Proceed ahead to a stile by an iron gate; turn right along a lane and take the footpath right just beyond Barretts Farm.

3. Cross a stile, keep right-handed along field edge to a stile, then go over a plank bridge to a further stile into a field. Turn left following markers to the end of the hedge, then proceed straight ahead across a large field to an arrowed footbridge across a stream. Turn left, then right over a stile and keep left-handed along the field edge towards farm buildings (Tearden Farm). Cross two stiles, a gate and further stiles by a barn before reaching a lane. Turn right follow the lane for about ½ mile to a sharp left-hand bend. then bear right onto a farm road and pass through Hamden Farm. Cross a stile flanking a metal gate and follow waymarked track across a field to another stile and gate, then keep right-handed along field edge to a bridge and stile onto a track.

4. Continue along the track to a road and take the lane opposite, signposted Smarden. Where the lane bears left, climb the waymarked stile right and cross the field to a further stile and gate. Proceed ahead towards farm buildings, cross a brick bridge and immediately take the re-directed stile and path on the left to head for iron gates and marker ahead. Maintain direction towards Smarden church to a stile and pass through a small housing estate to the village road. Cross over, enter the churchyard via a gate, then keep left of the church to a gate onto a lane. Keep ahead, passing the magnificent Cloth Hall on the left and remain on the lane soon to rejoin your outward route back to the inn.

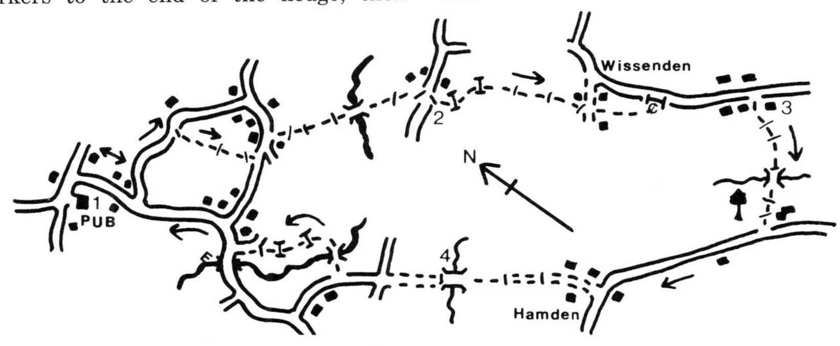

Walk No. 31

# The Spotted Dog, Smart's Hill

This picturesque white painted brick and weather boarded freehouse dates from 1520 and is set well back from the lane, hidden by mature trees and shrubs. It is justifiably a popular summer destination as the far-reaching views from the peaceful split-level terrace and garden – some 20 miles across the Medway Valley and Penshurst village – are quite magnificent. The unusual pub name arose from a mistake during the repainting of the pub sign. It was to represent the coat of arms of the Sydney family who resided at Penshurst Place, but a short-sighted painter mistook the leopard on the family crest for a spotted hunting dog. Four blazing log fires – one a huge inglenook – draw customers in on cold winter days, when they can relax in the charming series of inter-connecting rooms. Low ceilings, a wealth of timbering and wood panelling, quarry tiled and oak boarded floors and a delightful rustic mix of furniture characterise the snug interior.

Real ales served on hand pump include Larkins, Harveys Sussex and Spotty Dog – a best bitter brewed for the pub, and a regularly changing guest beer plus local Penshurst wines.

As well as the welcoming ambience and idyllic views, the pub is generally bustling with people seeking one of the good bar meals on offer here. Food Service is available Monday to Saturday 12 noon till 2.30 pm and 6 till 9 pm Sunday12 till 6 pm and includes a warming soup, pâtés, open sandwiches, ploughman's, salads, pies, and a range of pasta and rice dishes. A more extensive choice of meals is chalked up on six blackboards, which may list Lancashire hotpot, pork steak in cider and apple sauce, lamb and fresh tarragon and wine casserole, creamy pheasant casserole with pistachio nuts, bacon and garlic, venison sausages and navarin of lamb. Vegetarian meals may include tomato and fresh basil pie whilst the pudding board may feature honey and walnut pudding, lemon meringue pie and apple and apricot crumble.

Weekday opening times are from 11 till 11 pm, Sunday 12 noon till 10.30 pm.

Children are welcome away from the bar and dogs on a lead only.

Telephone: 01892 870253.

Hamlet and pub are situated just off the B2188 between Penshurst and Fordcombe, 5 miles north-west of Tunbridge Wells. Postcode: TN11 8EP.

Approx. distance: 4½ miles. OS Map No. 147 TQ 522/420.

The pub has a good car park across the lane.

*A scenic easy going ramble through the River Medway and Eden Valleys incorporating the attractive village of Penshurst with its fine manor house. Penshurst Place built between 1340 and 1345 and enlarged in later centuries is perfectly preserved and displays extensive collections of furniture, tapestries and paintings. There is a splendid chestnut-beamed hall, a toy museum and magnificent formal gardens (open late March to early October).*

1. On leaving the pub turn left along the lane, pass the old chapel and take the waymarked path left downhill beside a house to a stile. Continue downhill to a further stile and B-road, then turn left and shortly to cross over onto the arrowed path along a field edge in front of cottages to an unmetalled track. Turn right and follow it into Nashes Farm.
2. Keep left (can be muddy) between barns and farmhouses and soon bear right onto a wide hedged track which ends at a field. Turn left along its edge, pass into a further field, then keep right-handed on a defined path and soon walk beside the River Medway. Bear right into another field, pass an old pillbox, then proceed across a field on a worn path to rejoin the river bank. Cross the footbridge over the river and bear left around a field edge to join a grassy track in the far left-hand corner. Turn left then with Penshurst and valley views follow it to a B-road.
3. Turn left, cross the Medway and follow the footway into Penshurst. Keep ahead at the junction in the village centre, passing the Stores and garage, then bear right beyond the school along The Warren. Follow the metalled drive into Warren Farm. Pass a barn on your left and join a grassy path to a stile. Keep right-handed along the field edge on a defined path down to a further stile, then bear half-right to cross a footbridge over the River Eden. Continue beside a fence to another stile, cross pasture on a worn path to a gate, then follow field edge to climb a stile flanking a gate onto the driveway to Salmans Farm.
4. Turn left down the drive passing Harden Cottage on your left and where it turns sharp left go ahead on a footpath into woods. On reaching a lane turn right for 300 yards then turn left on an arrowed path up some stone steps through scrub into a field. Continue ahead on defined path towards a house and cross stile in fencing beyond the garden and bear diagonally right across two fields and stiles to an un-metalled drive. Turn right to a lane by the Bottle House Inn and turn left, then keep right at the second junction back to the pub.

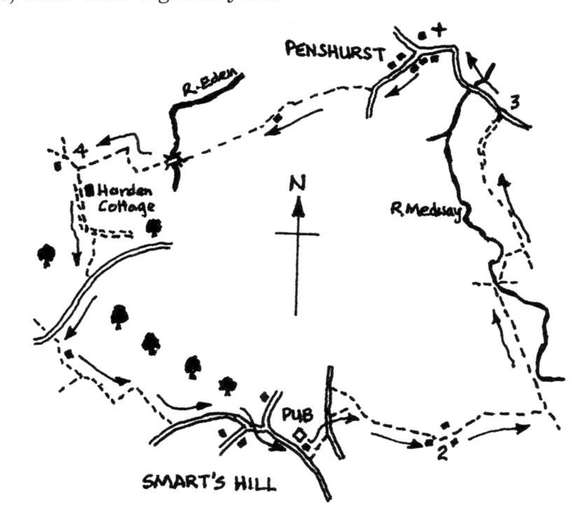

**Walk No. 32**

# The Compasses, Sole Street, Crundale

Nestling in a tiny hamlet within a web of narrow lanes in rolling countryside, this largely unspoilt white painted 500-year-old cottage has in its time been a religious premises and a carpenter's house before becoming an ale house. Beyond its flower-decked façade lies a rustic heavily beamed bar with a part stone and bare-boarded floors, two huge brick fireplaces and an assortment of simple furniture, including pine pews, tapestry covered stools and cut-away barrel seats. Separate games/children's room and large L shaped garden room with dark wood tables and chairs. Splendid lawned garden with picnic benches and play equipment including bat and trap to keep restless youngsters amused. Lovely views across pasture.

The pub is yet another freehouse acquired by Shepherd Neame the ales on offer include Master Brew and a changing second from the SN stable.

Food times are 12 noon till 2.30 pm (Sunday 3 pm) and 6 till 9 pm. The menu aims at "traditional country style" and is all home-cooked and sourced from local ingredients in season. Pan fried scallops with a rocket pesto and black pudding salad or potted confit of Gressingham duck with orange zest served with bread are just two lunchtime starters followed by braised rabbit, cider and root vegetable hot pot with sweet potato and leeks and lambs liver, bacon and caramelized onions on mashed potato with gravy. Examples of snacks are baguettes with a choice of four fillings including a vegetarian option, omelettes and ploughman's. There is a choice of three roasts on Sundays. Puddings include apple pie, treacle tart and banoffee pie, and honey, cinnamon and rhubarb crumble served with vanilla ice-cream. Children have their own menu.

Opening times are from 12 noon till 3 pm and 6 till 11 pm (Monday closed all day). Sunday 12 noon till 6 pm

Dogs on leads are welcome.

Telephone: 01277 700300. thecompassesinn@live.com

## Walk No. 32

Isolated hamlet on narrow lane off Petham to Waltham road 3½ miles off the B2068 south of Canterbury. Postcode: CT4 7ES.

Approx. distance of walk: 5 miles. OS Map No. 137 TR 095/493.

The pub has its own car park.

*A peaceful, gently and easy going, undulating walk along a defined by-way across the crest of the Crundale Downs, affording unspoilt countryside views and through open farmland.*

1. From the pub turn right along the lane, disregard the lane off to the left beyond Sole Cottages and proceed gently downhill to a waymarked track on your left. Follow the track between fields and shortly enter a woodland fringe on a path. At a junction of four paths turn left and follow the narrow path to a lane. Turn left uphill to Crundale Church.
2. Take the waymarked by-way beside the grassy parking area, pass through a gate and proceed along a delightful path along the rest of Crundale Downs with splendid unspoilt views across rolling downland. Beyond a metal gate, follow the earth bridleway into Towns Wood. Emerge and gently descend to a junction of tracks. Turn left uphill, the track becomes metalled as you enter the hamlet of Hassell Street.
3. Pass a house – once The Woodmans Arms – then just beyond Penang Lodge, take the arrowed path left along a grassy track into an open field. Proceed straight across, your path becomes defined and leads to a stile (yellow arrow). Keep right-handed along a fence and turn right trough a gateway on reaching woodland. Follow a grassy track to a gate and enter the wood. Shortly, turn left onto another track, then at a T-junction turn right and climb a gate into pasture.
4. Keep ahead and pass through a gate onto the driveway to Ashenfield Farm. Pass in front of the farmhouse, then keep right through a gate to follow a track between outbuildings. On entering a vast open field, continue straight ahead through the centre of the field. Cross a grassy track, maintain direction towards the field corner beside woodland to a stile. Bear half-right across pasture to a stile and turn left along a lane. Finally turn left at a crossroads for the ¼ mile walk back to the pub.

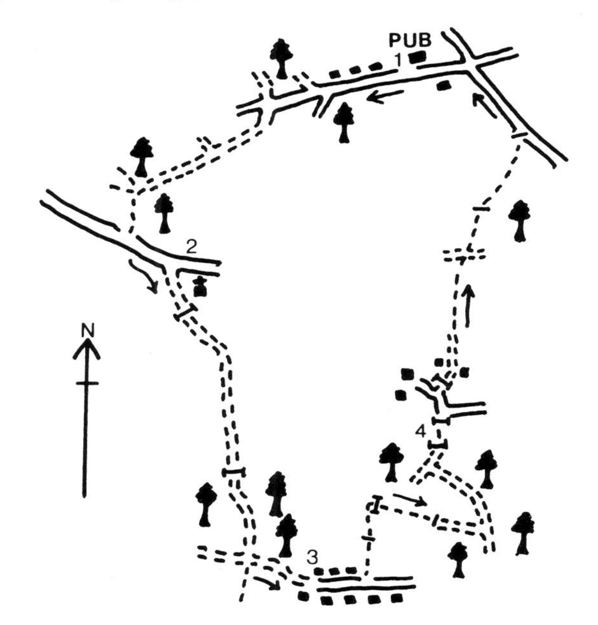

Walk No. 33

# The Plough, Stalisfield Green

This magnificent building is beautifully placed high up on the North Downs, nestling beside a green in a peaceful unspoilt hamlet and enjoys far-reaching views across the Swale to the Isle of Sheppey. Originally a galleried Wealden Hall House built in the 14th-century, it was a farmhouse prior to becoming a pub in 1745. Immaculately maintained outside and in the two beamed bars, the light and airy garden room and the cosy separate restaurant are tastefully furnished with an assortment of antique tables and chairs. Candles top the tables and various watercolours, prints and old photographs line the walls, while local hops adorn the beams and exposed upright timbers. Two open brick fireplaces warm this most attractive country pub.

This welcoming freehouse dispenses only Kentish ales which are changed frequently so think Shepherd Neame, Larkins, Goacher's and Westerham. Also available are Kentish wheat beer, Kentish lager and Kentish oyster stout on draught.

Food service is Tuesday to Friday 12 noon till 2.30 pm and 6.30 till 9 pm, Saturday 12 noon till 9 pm and Sunday 12 noon till 4 pm. Monday pub closed all day. Home-cooked food is a popular attraction here. The choice of dishes is excellent and the standard is high with the pub winning a 'best restaurant in Kent' award in 2008 and 'best pub in Kent' in the same year. In 2009 it was a finalist in the Countryside Alliance Local Food awards. The pub produces its own traditional bacon and sausages, bakes its own bread and makes its own ice-cream and you will find the free rangers roaming the garden. Dishes range from simple pub classics like homemade steamed steak and ale suet pudding to more elaborate lamb and pork dishes. During the winter months The Plough cold smoke much of its produce in its own traditional cold smoker imparting a delicate smoky flavour to a vast array of ingredients.

Opening times are Tuesday to Friday 12 noon till 3 pm and 6 till 11 pm, Saturday 12 noon till 12 pm and Sunday 12 noon till 9 pm.

Children are welcome and have their own menu. Dogs must be kept on a lead at all times.

Telephone: 01795 890256.

Village lies 2½ miles off the A20 Ashford to Maidstone road, signposted 1 mile north-west of Charing. Postcode: ME13 0HY.

Approx. distance of walk: 6 miles. OS Map No. 137 TQ 954/530

The pub has its own car park.

*A splendid rural walk across the back slope of the North Downs, exploring peaceful farmland and woodland paths. Excellent views south across Charing and the Stour Valley and north over the Swale to the Isle of Sheppey. Some of the field paths may be hard going, especially if ploughed.*

1. From the pub cross the green and main village lane onto the narrow lane close to the village hall and follow it to a T-junction. Turn right and almost immediately climb the waymarked stile left, then keep to the left-hand fence downhill to stile proceeding woodland. Continue downhill on the defined path (yellow markers on trees), keep ahead at a crossing of paths and ascend to the woodland fringe. Continue straight across an open field – path marked by sticks – pass through a narrow chestnut copse and bear slightly left on a worn path to join a track beside a copse to a lane, opposite Court Lodge.

2. Cross the lane, turn right through the gate into the churchyard, then bear left to a further arrowed wooden gate and follow grassy path to a stile in the corner of the churchyard. Turn left along field edge, passing silos and barns and gently descend to woodland. At a crossroads of paths on the woodland fringe, turn right with blue arrow and keep to the established waymarked path (can be muddy) to a lane. Turn right gradually descend, then take the arrowed stile left to follow a narrow path along the edge of scrub and into trees to a stile and driveway. Turn right and remain on this pitted track to a T-junction with a metalled lane. Bear right, cross over disregarding footpath left and enter a lane called "The Wynd". Take the tarmac driveway right beside Mill House Lodge (splendid views left), pass through a gate and proceed to a further swing gate just beyond a converted windmill.

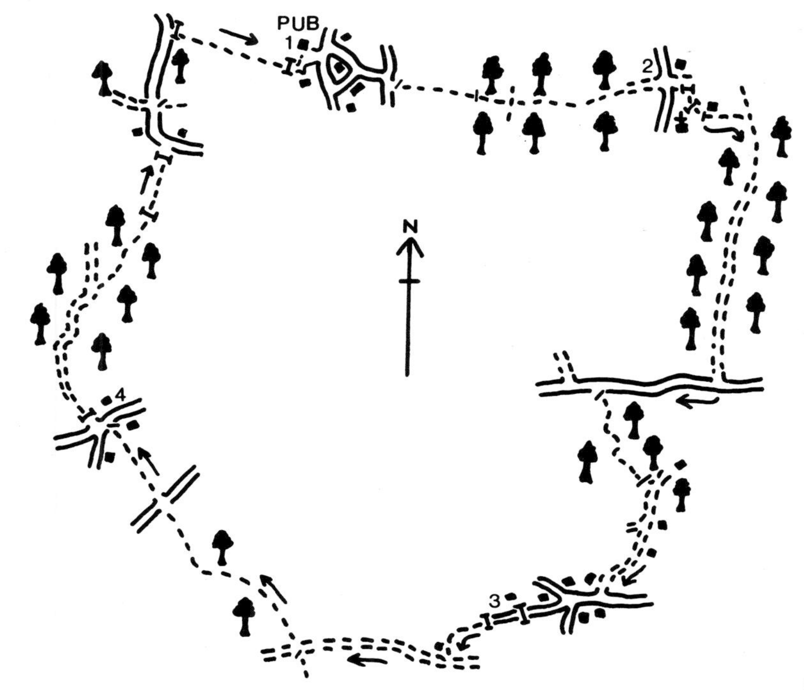

3. Follow yellow waymarker, pass beside a further gate and keep to the well worn path that steeply descends off the North Downs to a track. – The Pilgrims/North Downs Way. Turn right along this fine hedged bridleway affording good views, then on reaching a stile on your left bear right into an open field (yellow topped post). Head diagonally left steeply uphill, soon to follow the tree lined edge to the field corner and marker post. Enter adjacent field, proceed across field to the edge of trees, then bear right on a worn path to a lane. Cross over and maintain direction to pass through a wide gap in the hedge in right-hand corner of the field. Cut across the corner of the next field towards a bungalow to reach a stile and lane.

4. Keep ahead across the road junction, climb the waymarked stile flanking a gate near the bungalow driveway and follow trackway right through mixed woodland. Shortly, bear sharp right, then left with track onto a wide grassy clearing. The track soon becomes tree-lined again, but in a few yards bear off right with narrow worn path (not waymarked), uphill through woodland to a gate. Turn left along the field edge track, pass through a gate and turn left along a quiet lane. Ignore arrowed stile on your right opposite a track, pass brick cottages to the left and right, then at the end of a copse turn right onto a waymarked footpath through a wooden gate. Keep to this grassy path between a hedgerow and fence, eventually reaching a gate beside the pub garden. Turn left for the pub car park.

Converted windmill on top of the North Downs near Charing

# The Tiger Inn, Stowting

This remote rural retreat lies in the scattered hamlet of Stowting, which nestles in some delightful countryside at the foot of the North Downs. Parts of the inn date back to the 16th-century and despite changes to the interior over the years it has lost none of its character, remaining traditional and unpretentious in both atmosphere and layout. The cosy front bar has exposed brickwork and wood panelling, bare floorboards are strewn with colourful rugs and an open log fire warms either end of the room. Rustic cushioned chairs, wall pews and candle-topped tables furnish both this homely bar and the further connecting dining room to the rear. To the front of the pub a Russian vine clings to a pergola and covers the terrace area which has picnic tables and a summer barbecue.

This popular free house offers an excellent range of real ales from Shepherd Neame, Harveys, Fullers, Goacher's and Adnams plus Biddenden cider on pump.

There is a good choice of home-cooked bar food from opening time to 9 pm on weekdays, 9.30 pm Saturday and 8 pm Sunday. Listed on a blackboard will be soup, devilled whitebait and duck and port pate among the range of starters. Main dishes include tandoori chicken, cock-a-leekie pie, minty leg of lamb steak, steak, kidney and mushroom pie served with vegetables, chilli, lasagne, trout and a selection of sandwiches, ploughman's and stuffed jacket potatoes. Vegetarian main meals range from vegetable korma to vegetable and basil pie.

Opening hours are Mondays 4 pm till midnight, Tuesday closed all day, Wednesday to Saturday 12 noon till midnight, Sunday 12 noon till 10.30 pm.

Children and dogs are welcome in the pub and on the patio.

There are three double rooms available to overnight visitors.

Telephone: 01303 862130.

## Walk No. 34

Village signposted off the B2068, 2½ miles north of junction 11 of the M20 Westenhanger, near Hythe. Postcode: TN25 6BA.

Approx. distance of walk: 3½ miles. OS Map No. 138 TQ 120/414.

The inn has its own car park to the rear and a few spaces at the front.

*A short, level walk across farmland paths and along a quiet narrow country lane. Good scenic views along the North Downs. Fairly easy going, but some ploughed fields can make boots heavy after wet weather.*

1. From the pub cross the lane and waymarked stile opposite and follow the narrow path beside a fence to a stile beside a gate and turn right along a lane. Just past Chestnut Cottage, cross the arrowed stile left and bear diagonally right across pasture to a further stile. Cross a small plank bridge and another stile then turn left along the field edge (yellow marker) to a stile. Maintain left-hand course beside a tree-lined hedge and shortly bear right along a defined grassy break between fields uphill towards a church. Pass to the left of double-gates onto a lane.
2. Turn right, pass Hopton Court and cross a stile on your left and proceed ahead to a gate. Turn right along the field edge with yellow arrow to a stile in the field corner. Keep right-handed, then on reaching the gap into the adjacent field, bear diagonally left across the open field, looking out for a plank bridge and stile in the tree-lined hedge. Continue ahead to a stile and lane.
3. Turn right, pass Smeads Farm into the hamlet of Broad Street and ignore junctions to left and right. Pass the Black Horse and shortly bear right into a field and follow the left-hand edge round to a stile. Proceed half-right to a further stile and continue ahead across pasture towards a group of trees. Pass to the left of the trees to a stile and keep ahead to another stile. Turn right around the field edge, looking out for a footbridge across a stream in the trees on your right. Cross a stile, turn left and cross another stile in the field corner. Keep left-handed along the hedge, then proceed across a field to a stile into a further field and bear diagonally right on the defined path, eventually reaching a stile and lane at a junction. Head across a grassy triangle and follow the lane for Stowting back to the pub.

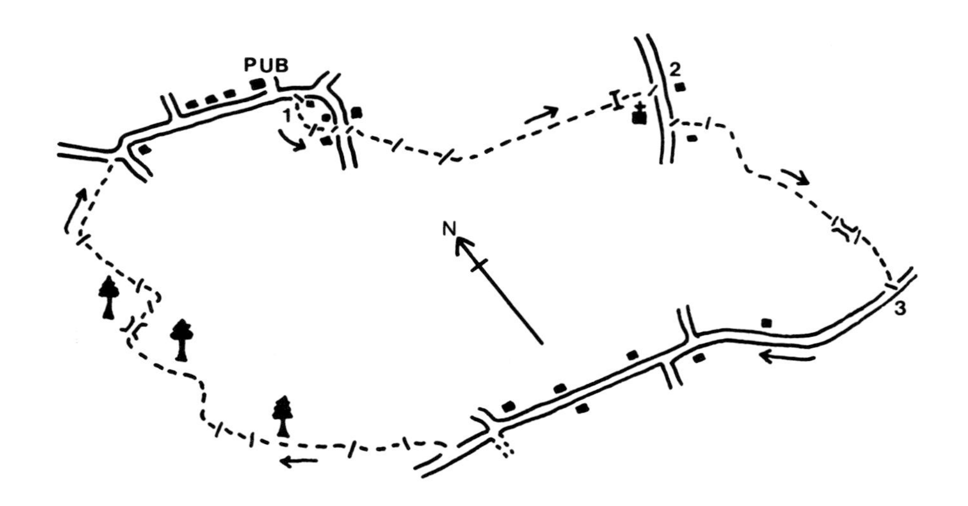

# The Swan, Sutton Valence

The village of Sutton Valence is perched on top of the Greensand ridge and commands superb views across the Weald. Among its tiered streets stand some interesting old houses, one of the oldest being an impressive half-weather-boarded Swan Inn, which is believed to date from the 12th-century and is typical Kentish-style building. It is possibly one of the oldest inns in the country reputed to have been a pub since 1348 but acquired its licence in 1467. The interior is that of an unchanged, traditional village inn with two homely bars – public and lounge. The unpretentious carpeted lounge has a heavily beamed ceiling, an attractive bay window with bench seats overlooking the village street, a small brick fireplace and various small stools. In 1927 a fire, which began beneath a beam in the upstairs fireplace, seriously damaged the outer wall of this bar. The unspoilt public bar boasts a huge inglenook fireplace with winter log fire, exposed black painted upright timbers and is simply furnished with stools, wall bench seating and dartboard.

Enterprise Inns own this friendly pub which serves well kept Young's Bitter, Harveys Sussex and Woodforde's Wherry on handpump

Food is served from 12 noon till 3 pm, Sunday 4 pm and 6 till 9 pm. The restaurant menu lists soup, home-cooked ham, egg and chips, roasted breast of pigeon with beetroot puree and baby leaf salad, whole camembert baked in the box (ideal for sharing), Caesar salad with or without chicken, beer battered cod and chips, local Kentish sausages served with creamy mash and parsnip crisps, caramelized onions and gravy, steak and ale pie plus good value snacks such as baguettes and freshly cut sandwiches. Evening fare will include various steaks, grilled gammon and fish dishes, all produce is sourced locally. Fine weather alfresco eating can be enjoyed on the rear terraced lawned garden.

Opening times are from 12 noon till 11 pm, Friday/Saturday close at midnight, Sunday 10.30 pm.

Well behaved children are welcome so to are dogs.

Telephone: 01622 843212.

## Walk No. 35

Village is located on a ridge, just off the A272 between Maidstone and Tenterden, 5½ miles south-west of Maidstone. Postcode: ME17 3AJ.

Approx. distance of walk: 5 miles. OS Map No. 137 TQ 813/492.

Park in the village street outside the inn.

*A peaceful scenic walk along the greensand escarpment with panoramic views across the Weald of Kent. Well waymarked along the Greensand Way returning along gently undulating field paths which can be wet and muddy underfoot. Sutton Valence is a pretty village with an old ruined castle and a notable public school which dominates the village.*

1. From the pub turn left, follow the raised pavement uphill out of the village and walk along the (Greensand Way) to a cross-roads. Bear left to a waymarked stile and head straight across an open field on a worn path, crossing a farm track before bearing slightly right to a stile and junction of lanes. Proceed ahead along the lane passing East Sutton Church and the entrance to the Open Prison to a T-junction. Climb the stile opposite, head downhill on a grassy track and pass through a gate. Ascend through pasture to a gate to the left of a cottage and turn left up a lane.
2. Shortly, turn right with Greensand Way markers beside Morry House and proceed through the top of a hop field and an orchard. Soon join an established trackway with fine views and head towards Ulcombe Church. Pass farm buildings, and walk along the driveway beside the churchyard to a lane and turn right downhill into Ulcombe village. Beyond The Harrow, take the waymarked path beside the school and play area into a field. Keep right-handed around the field edge to cross a plank bridge into a further field. Turn left along the field edge parallel to the brook, then just beyond some trees pass through a field entrance and go right-handed along a hedgerow to a stile. Continue through a pasture and join a track leading to a lane.
3. Cross over and bear half-left across pasture on a defined path to a fence stile and plank bridge over a stream. Head uphill beside fence to a stile and lane. Cross the stile opposite, keep left-handed, then just beyond a line of trees bear diagonally left to a gate in the field corner. Head slightly left uphill to a stile and enter woodland. Pass through woodland fringe with lake to your right, cross a stile and maintain direction across pasture, over a low fence and along the field edge to a stile and lane.
4. Turn left, then shortly right (waymarked) through a gate. Proceed through a further gate, keep right uphill to a fence stile and continue to a lane. Turn right steeply uphill, pass Boyton Court Cottages and soon take the metalled drive left, opposite Boyton Court. At a fork of ways, bear slightly right onto a defined path at the base of a steep concrete road and soon pass to the side of a gate onto a metalled lane. Proceed ahead, pass Sutton Place and keep left at a fork to follow the lane past Sutton Castle back to the village pub.

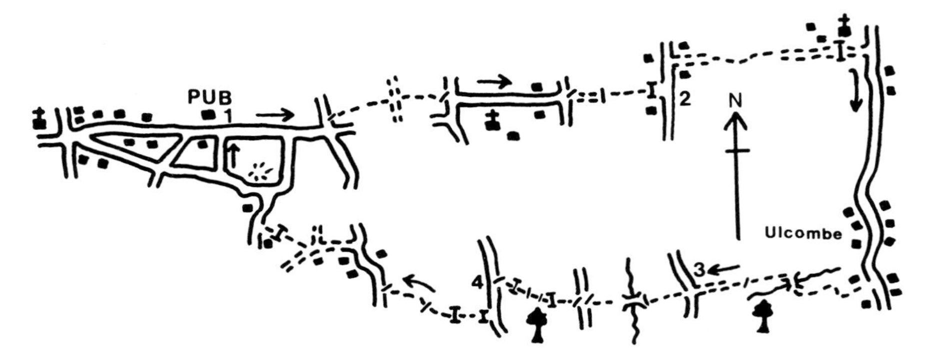

# The Fox and Hounds, Toy's Hill

The isolated and homely Fox and Hounds, set 800 feet up on the greensand ridge – is the highest pub in Kent amid 200 acres of National Trust woodland

In our first report on this inn in 1994 it was very much a locals' pub and many people and organisations at that time campaigned against its refurbishment and enlargement by Friary Meux. The inn then changed hands and became part of the Green King estate who did refurbish and extend it. The manager said (in 2010) that it is a pub in name but a restaurant by trade. Fortunately they still welcome walkers, children and dogs. The welcome includes real fires in winter and the large woodland garden makes for pleasant alfresco lunch in the summer.

They do serve real ales presently Green King IPA, Abbot Ale and Morland Original Bitter.

An imaginative sandwich menu is available Monday to Friday from 12 noon till 3 pm with main meals from local produce available 12 noon till 2 pm, Saturday 2.30 pm and Sunday 3 pm, evenings 6 till 9.30 pm. Dishes range from moules mariniere and griddled peach and Parma ham tart to kipper pate with a hint of chilli, lemon rocket salad and warm dates wrapped in smoked bacon with a corn salad. There are platters to share and imaginative salads. Shirley's home made cream teas are available Saturday and Sunday from 3 till 6 pm. Meal deals Tuesday to Friday evenings.

Tuesday to Saturday open all day 11.30 am to 11 pm, Sunday 11.30 am to 10.30 pm. Closed on Mondays from 14th September till Bank Holiday Monday.

Dogs are welcome in the bar area but not the restaurant.

Telephone: 01732 750328.

## Walk No. 36

The hamlet lies high up on the wooded greensand ridges between the A25 at Brasted (signposted) and the B2042 near Four Elms, 5 miles west of Sevenoaks. Postcode: TN16 1QG.

Approx. distance of walk: 4 miles. OS Map No. 147 TQ 471/520.

Parking is limited at the pub, it is best to park in the large National Trust car park (free) which is located a few hundred yards south along the lane.

*A most delightful undulating walk across the greensand ridge incorporating National Trust woodland paths, the Greensand Way and a peaceful lane. Glorious far-reaching views and the opportunity to visit Chartwell, once the home of Sir Winston Churchill. Also worth a visit nearby are Emmetts Garden (NT) and Quebec House (NT) and Squerryes Court, both located in Westerham.*

1. From the NT car park locate the information board in the left-hand corner, disregard The Greensand Way path and take the footpath marked by a red, green and orange painted post. At T-junction of paths keep left passing memorial stone and the old site of Weardale Manor and remain on the main path, eventually bearing off right downhill with the red marked footpath. At a crossing of paths proceed straight ahead, leaving the red route, downhill to a stile on the woodland fringe. Keep left-handed alongside a fence to a further stile and soon join a track in front of old oasts and cottage (Outridge Farm).
2. In a little way bear off left to a stile, waymarked French Street, then descend through pasture on a worn path to cross a double stile and footbridge in the valley bottom. Keep left to a stile, then climb steeply to a further stile and lane in the hamlet of French Street. Turn left, then right along the driveway to a house called Mannings Wood, joining the Greensand Way. Proceed along the hedged trackway beside the property, then on reaching a metalled drive turn immediately left with GW marker. Continue through woodland (good views), eventually reaching a lane.
3. Cross over and remain on the narrow Greensand Way path, downhill with Chartwell soon visible to your left to a reach a stile and lane. Go straight across, climb uphill, then at GW marker post bear off left to follow permitted rhododendron fringed path beyond a wooden barrier. Splendid views across Chartwell to the Weald beyond. Pass beside a further barrier, keep left at a T-junction of paths and turn right along the lane, passing Chartwell Cottage. Shortly turn left along the driveway to Chartwell Farm, signposted Puddledock.
4. Pass to the left of the farmhouse and beside some oasts to a kissing gate, and then keep right along a concrete farm track, soon to cross a stile beside a wooden gate. Proceed on this delightful path to a stile and lane. Turn left and remain on this peaceful lane which climbs steeply into the hamlet of Toy's Hill, affording fine views. Just before reaching a T-junction, take the arrowed path left beyond the telephone box and gradually ascend into the National Trust woodland. Keep right, pass beside a wooden barrier, then at a crossing of paths turn right with GW marker and follow the defined path back to the car park.

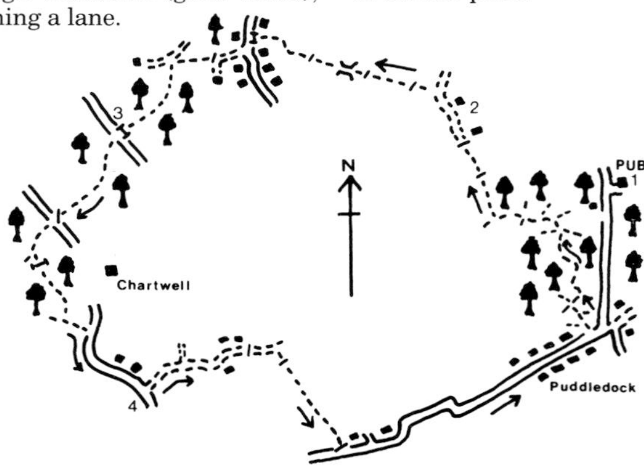

# The White Rock Inn, Under River

The village of Under River dates back to the Magna Carta and its unusual name derives from the Anglo-Saxon word 'rither', meaning hill or escarpment. Over the years this changed to 'river', thus the name literally means 'under the hill'. Tucked in the heart of the village is the White Rock Inn, a neat red brick building dating from 1820 with a single storey clapboard extension. The original building houses the cosy small saloon bar which features brick and stone walls, beams, a woodblock floor, padded wall bench seating and dark wood tables and chairs. Adjoining this bar is the attractive restaurant with fresh flowers on the tables. The much larger and livelier public bar fills the weatherboard extension and contains the dartboard and pool table. More traditional pub games can be played, namely chess, cribbage, draughts and shove ha'penny and located in the garden is a bat and trap pitch and a boule/pentanque pitch.

The real ale selection in this lovely freehouse includes Harveys Sussex, Websters Yorkshire Bitter and a guest.

An interesting choice of bar meals is chalked up on a large blackboard. Specials might include hot grilled goats cheese served on a crouton with Black Forest ham and king scallops wrapped in bacon, served with garlic butter followed by a rack of English lamb or crispy roast duck. Served from 12 noon till 3 pm and 6.30 till 9.30 pm (9 pm Sunday) favourite snacks include generously filled baps, ploughman's and basket meals and the restaurant has an appetising menu featuring local produce and traditional Sunday roasts.

Opening times are from 11.30 am till 4 pm and 6 till 11 pm, Sunday 12 noon till 10.30 pm

Children are most welcome in the bar and restaurant, dogs in the garden only.

Telephone: 01732 833112.

## Walk No. 37

Village signposted off the B245 between Sevenoaks and Hildenborough. Postcode: TN15 05B.

Approx. distance of walk: 4 miles. OS Map No. 147 TQ 557/521.

Walkers are welcome to park in the large rear car park.

*A delightful walk exploring the Greensand Way along the high wooded and scenic ridge overlooking Tonbridge and the western edge of the Weald. Unrivalled views, well waymarked paths (some can be muddy) and close to the splendid National Trust properties of Knole Park and Ightham Mote (both open April – October).*

1. From the inn turn right along the lane and take the arrowed bridleway beside Valley Farm. Pass in front of a house named Black Charles – a listed historic building of Kent – and begin to climb steadily uphill on a splendid old route way. Just before a farm lane, turn right onto a path between renovated oasts and a house and continue the climb to the top of the ridge, on what can be a muddy, sunken path. Climb the stile on your right and follow narrow fenced path (greensand Way), with magnificent view to a lane.
2. Cross straight over a waymarked track, then at a fork of tracks keep left gently uphill, passing White Rock Farm on your right. Continue along a signed path which gently undulates through scrub and woodland – abundant birdlife – along the crest of the ridge. On reaching a lane turn left steeply uphill for a short distance and take the arrowed path right through the woodland fringe. Soon cross a stile into National Trust land of Ightham Mote and follow the narrow path to a further stile onto a track by a cottage.
3. Cross the waymarked stile on your right and proceed downhill across pasture to a further stile. Keep right-handed along the field-edge path, downhill across a small footbridge and follow the worn path slightly right to a stile beside a gate onto a lane. Turn right, then right again onto the driveway to Great Budds (waymarked). Keep right to stile flanking a gate, pass a pond, cross a further stile and continue on a track and later a defined path across an open field to two stiles. Maintain direction through pasture to a stile and across a farmyard to a gate. Keep right along the edge of woodland towards Under River House and cross a stile in the field corner. Follow the path right, then bear left between tall fir trees to the driveway and turn right, soon to reach a lane. Bear right, shortly climb an arrowed stile left and head straight across pasture to a stile. Turn half-left with arrow and soon pick up a defined east-west grassy path to a stile. Continue across two stiles, then keep left-handed alongside trees to a stile and lane in Under River. Turn left back to the pub.

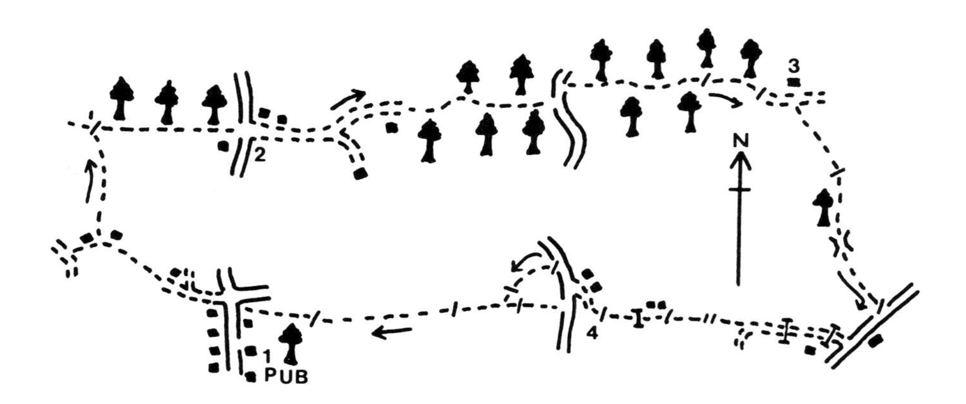

# The Harrow Inn, Warren Street

Situated north of Lenham Village high up on the North Downs in an isolated hamlet, this large, part traditional weather boarded old 17th-century inn was once a forge and rest house for travellers along the ancient Pilgrims Way. Over recent years the inn has been refurbished to a high standard with a conservatory dining room looking out onto a patio, garden and waterfall area. The bar is traditional, with oak floors, open log fire, decorated with water jugs, mirrors and nick-nacks of a bygone age.

The Harrow is a privately owned free house offering a range of beers, wines and spirits including a fine selection of malt whiskies. Real ales on hand pump are usually two brews from Goachers and a guest.

Food service is daily from 12 noon till 2 pm and 7 till 9 pm, Sunday 12 to 3 pm. A varied menu is available ranging from sandwiches and baguettes, bar meals and more substantial offerings including beef, chicken and fish dishes, pasta and a selection of vegetarian dishes. A full roast lunch is available on Sundays.

Opening times Tuesday to Friday 12.30 till 3 pm and 6 till 11 pm all day Saturday and 12 noon till 4 pm on Sunday. Closed Mondays.

Families are welcome.There are two outside patio areas and dogs are welcome in the bar (with owners on a lead) with a bowl of Adnams Ale and a Bonio

12 comfortable and tastefully decorated rooms. For a small charge dogs can be accommodated.

Telephone: 01622 859846.

## Walk No. 38

Hamlet is located on top of the North Downs, 1 mile north of the A20 between Maidstone and Charing, just east of Lenham. Postcode: ME17 2ED

Approx. distance of walk: 4½ miles. OS Map No. 137 TQ 927/529.

The pub has a good large car park and customers are invited to arrive early for a walk and return to 'Traditional hospitality'

*An enjoyable rural walk through farmland on the backslope of the North Downs, returning along the long-distance path – the North Downs Way/Pilgrims Way – a scenic and peaceful trackway that traverses the scarp slope of the Downs. At certain times of the year heavily ploughed fields can make the going difficult underfoot.*

1. Leave the inn, turn left along the lane, then where the road curves left bear off right at the footpath fingerpost into a large open field. Head diagonally left, then on reaching a trackway follow it right and keep ahead where it ends across a field to a stile preceding woodland. Pass through the wood and proceed straight on across the centre of a large field, between telegraph poles to a stile and lane, opposite Bleak Cottage.
2. Turn left, cross the lane and turn right along a track, passing The Bungalow and Pond Cottage. Pass a garage, go through a gate and shortly follow the waymarked path across the front of Woodside Green Cottage to a stile and junction of paths. Turn left along the field edge and beside a garden fence to a lane. Turn left, pass High Farm, then at the T-junction proceed straight across onto a waymarked path into an open field. Bear half left towards a building just visible in the trees and climb two stiles (can be overgrown) onto a driveway. Bear right, then left across a stile, or through the gap in the fence and descend diagonally left across a field (good views) to a gate in the far corner.
3. Turn left onto the North Downs Way, keep ahead along the lane and soon bear off left onto a metalled lane, beyond a row of cottages. Shortly pass trough a gate onto a grassy track, following the North Downs Way beneath the war memorial cross etched in the chalk hillside to a gate. Continue on the hedged path to a lane and turn left uphill. Disregard the first arrowed path right, take the second waymarked path (NDW) and remain on this path to a narrow lane. Turn left steeply uphill, eventually turning left at a T-junction back to the inn.

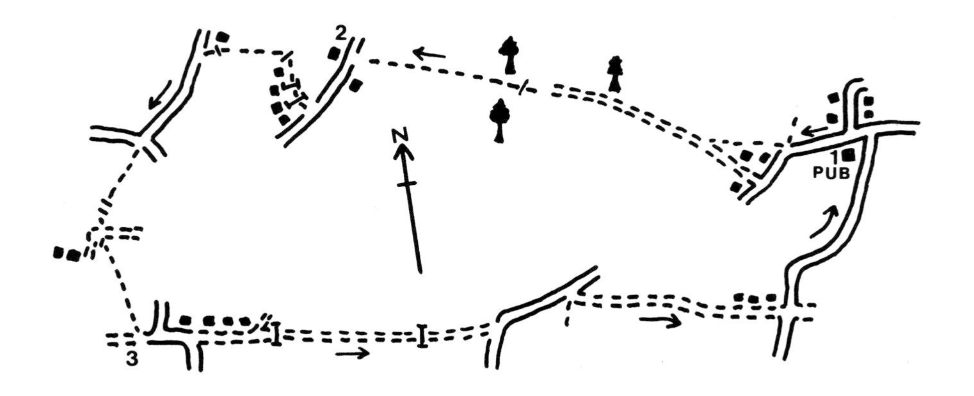


The sketch maps in this book are not necessarily to scale but have been drawn to show maximum amount of detail.

# The Woolpack, Warehorne

The handsome photogenic Woolpack dates from the mid 15th-century when it began life as a farmhouse. In the 18th and 19th centuries, then an inn, it was a local centre for the wool trade from which it derived its name. There is evidence that it was closely associated with 'owling', the smuggling of wool to avoid the excise. This activity is depicted on the inn sign. Its raised position made it a good look out point and there was a tunnel between the pub and St Matthew's Church opposite. It is also renowned for its ghosts, a young girl, a clergyman and Fred, a smuggler, all flitting about along the tunnel no doubt.

This is a very welcoming and comfortable pub with log fires in winter. In 2010 new management took over this free house and were working hard to build up the pub's reputation as a dining venue – the words "gastro pub" were uttered, but as the pub is already popular with walkers, they were also contemplating offering a "walker's lunch". Details were still in gestation but this could involve parties ringing ahead to book from a limited menu, thereby minimising delay on arrival.

Food service is Wednesday to Saturday 12 noon till 2.30 pm, Friday and Saturday 7 till 9.30 pm and Sunday 12 noon till 6 pm. The policy is to use all fresh produce sourced locally, specialising in fresh fish, steak, game in season with vegetarian options. Snacks include a cheese board to share, homemade soup, olives and crudités.

Opening times are Wednesday to Friday 12 noon till 3 pm, Monday to Friday 6 till 11 pm, weekends 12 noon till 10.30 pm. At the time of writing the pub is closed at lunchtime on Mondays and Tuesday. On these days an alternative would be to use the Back Lion at Appledore which is en route.

Children are welcome and have their own menu; dogs are allowed in the snug but not the carpeted dining area.

Telephone: 01233 733888.

**Walk No. 39**

The pub is located in Church Road, Warehorne, a turning south off the B2067 between Kenardington and Hamstreet. Postcode: TN26 2LL.

Approx. distance of walk: 6½ miles. OS Map No. 125 TQ 990/350.

Park at the pub or in Church Road.

*A longish walk but easy going across farmland on the well signed Saxon Shore Way with the return beside the Royal Military Canal, where there is much bird life. If you follow the tradition of kissing gates then choose your companion wisely and pucker up as there are 17 such excuses to dally distributed along this walk.*

1. Turn right out of the pub and cross the road. After about 220 yards turn left into a lane and immediately right through the first kissing gate with Saxon Shore Way markers. Follow the marker direction across a field to the rear of a detached house on the right. Go through a kissing gate and then diagonally left to a small footbridge, keeping the low hedge on your left. Cross the bridge and continue on over another bridge, then a sleeper bridge and through a kissing gate. Maintain direction through another kissing gate beside a farm gate and make for a church at the top of the field. Keep to the left through the churchyard to another kissing gate at the top. Keep right past a large house and turn right past a waymark to yet one more kissing gate.

2. Route finding from here is quite clear as you just continue to follow the Saxon Shore Way markers for 2 miles to reach the B2080 road. Here turn left into Appledore, where you may be pleased to see The Black Lion pub on your left at the bottom of the village.

3. Continue down the hill past the church and just before the bridge turn left off the road through a kissing gate onto the path beside the Royal Military Canal. Now follow the canal for about 2½ miles through four further kissing gates. In sight of the railway bridge on your right cross a small stream on your left by footbridge opposite a waymark. Turn right over a stile from the footbridge and head across a field towards the church. Climb a stile into the churchyard, head right weaving your way through the headstones to the main path and cross the road back to The Woolpack

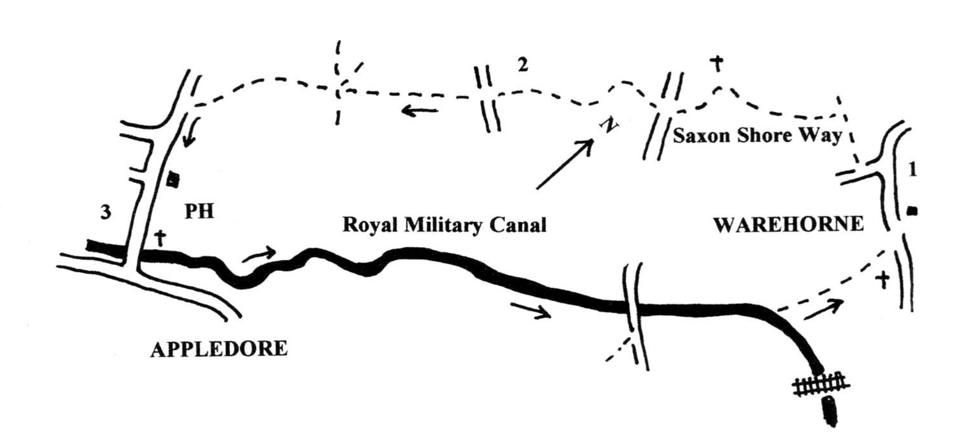

# The Tickled Trout, Wye

This neat, white-painted riverside building dates from about 1650 when it was used as a tannery with barges on the adjacent River Stour transporting the 'cured' skins to the ports. It became an inn during the Victorian era and was called the Queen Victoria or the Old Vic to the locals and visitors to the now abandoned Wye racecourse. During the 1970s it closed, the building soon becoming almost derelict. Since then it has been given a new lease of life, capitalising on the riverside setting and acquiring its present name from a tributary trout stream of the Great Stour. Decoration is rustic style with exposed brickwork, dark wood-panelled walls, stained glass panels, old beams, shelves of old bottles and other nick-nacks and a comfortable mix of modern pine tables, captains' chairs and padded wall bench seating. There is a delightful light and airy conservatory with floral curtains, cane furniture and views across the waterside lawn to the ancient stone bridge.

The inn is owned by Enterprise Inns with a selection of ales from five hand pumps dispensing such delights as Hopdemon from Ramsgate, Harveys Best, Timothy Taylor Landlord, Ringwood Best, Black Sheep and Hop Back Summer Lightning.

Good lunch time bar food, all home-cooked, is listed on a printed menu and a daily changing specials board. Available, Monday to Friday 12 till 2.30 and 6 till 9 pm all day at weekends. Dishes included jacket potatoes, sandwiches, ploughman's, fresh salads and hot dishes like steak and kidney pie, Cajun chicken, bubble and squeak, bangers and mash and a good selection of fresh fish dishes e.g. sea bass and salmon.

Opening times all day 11 am (12 noon Sunday) to 11 pm.

Children and dogs are welcome.

Telephone: 01233 812227.

### Walk No. 40

Wye is situated 1 mile off the A28, 3 miles north-east of Ashford. Postcode: TN25 5EB.

Approx. distance of walk: 4¾ miles. OS map No. 137 TQ 049/469.

The pub has a car park and parking is available at the Village Hall along the street.

*A most enjoyable and scenic ramble across the Wye Downs with superb views across the eastern Weald and Romney Marsh. The walk explores Wye Down Nature Reserve and returns along well waymarked field paths and tracks. One steep climb.*

1. From the pub turn left along the main village street, then turn left into Church Street and shortly cross Churchfield Way into the churchyard. Bear diagonally right with North Downs Way marker along a tarmac path, then bear left between allotments and Wye College buildings. Pass round the back of the college onto a road, then cross a further road following the North Downs Way fingerpost. Follow the college road, pass through a metal gate at its end onto a wide track towards the Downs. Cross a lane and head uphill to a gate preceding woodland.

2. Proceed steeply uphill on a narrow fenced path through trees to reach a lane. Turn right, gradually climb uphill, then cross a stile on your right and keep ahead to a stile beside a gate. Cross a further stile and turn left along the crest of the Downs, passing the crown shape monument etched into the chalk hillside. Continue along the left-hand fence with magnificent views to a gate and a metalled driveway.

3. Turn right, cross a road and stile into Wye Downs National Reserve. Follow the waymarked path onto Broad Down, cross a stile and shortly turn right through a small wooden gate. Proceed along a grassy path to the edge of the Downs and descend on a chalky zig-zag path, crossing two stiles to a lane.

4. Turn right, then in a few metres climb a stile on your left and proceed straight ahead across an open field to a waymarked stile. Keep left-handed on a grassy path, pass through a gateway, then bear left through a second gateway and turn right with yellow marker along the right hand edge of a field to a stile. Maintain direction, cross another stile beside a gate and follow the trackway to a further two stiles and cross a farm driveway. Climb a stile and continue along a track to a metalled lane and soon to pass Withersdane Hall on your right. Bear off left and join a narrow path beside playing fields, then cross a road onto a lane between houses back to the main village road. Turn left through the village back to the pub.

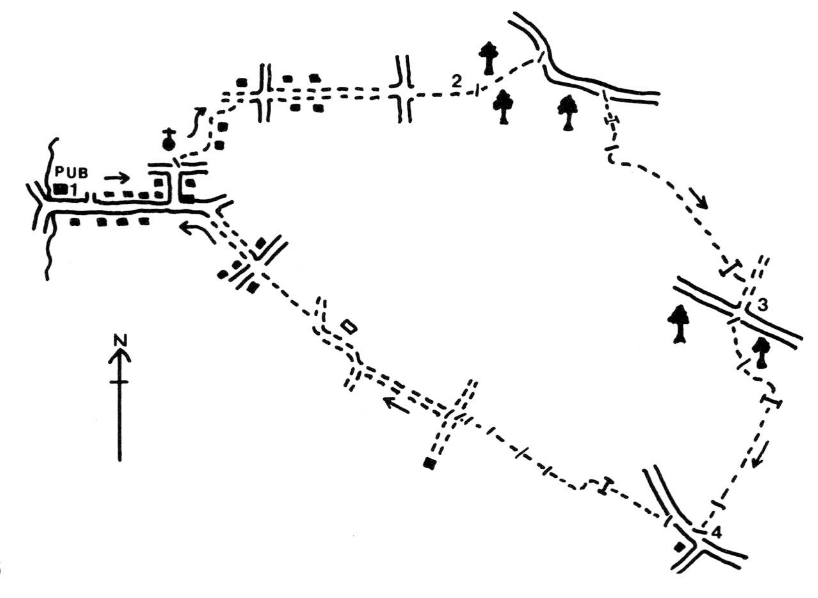